10.10

YEAR 2000
in easy steps

Brian Austin

COMPUTER STEP

In easy steps is an imprint of Computer Step
Southfield Road . Southam
Warwickshire CV33 OFB . England

Tel: 01926 817999 Fax: 01926 817005
http://www.computerstep.com

Notice of Liability
Every effort has been made to ensure that this book contains accurate
and current information. However, Computer Step and the author shall
not be liable for any loss or damage suffered by readers as a result of
any information contained herein.

Trademarks
All trademarks are acknowledged as belonging to their respective
companies.

Printed and bound in the United Kingdom

ISBN 1-84078-009-6

Contents

One Minute to Midnight!

It's one minute to midnight on December 31st, 1999. In the next sixty seconds, a momentous event is going to take place: the new century will be born followed closely by a new millennium. But in this book we're really concerned about the effects the change-over date will have on computers – including both hardware and software – and other date-reliant electronic devices right across the globe. In this chapter, we introduce two imaginary scenarios of what *could* happen if the Year 2000 problem is not addressed properly.

Covers

Chapter One

How to receive a 99-year phone bill

Let's create an imaginary scenario. You live in Birmingham, England. The exact location doesn't really matter: it could be in any city in any country across the globe.

The new millennium arrives amid the seasonal and new millennium celebrations. The air is electric with excitement: a new century dawns. Familiar sounds of people enjoying festivals and parties echoes across a small insignificant planet on the edge of an insignificant galaxy.

HANDY TIP This book is designed to be read either in a single session, or you can skim and scan to find the information you want quickly. Also, don't forget the margins: you'll find lots of really useful hints, tips, advice and 'linkers' to other relevant pages.

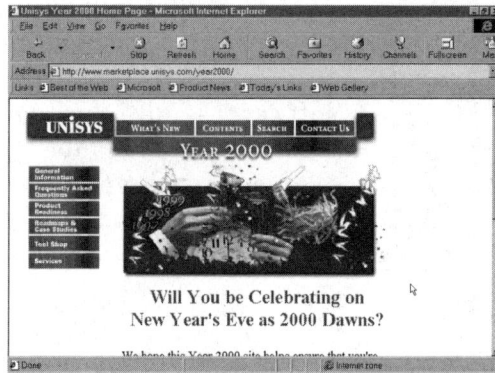

Amid the excitement, particularly for businesses, organisations and those individuals who use computer systems, there's also more than a hint of the FUD factor – Fear, Uncertainty and Doubt – as the dateline between the old and new millenniums changes. You can feel the tension!

HANDY TIP Although having great faith in human beings' capacity to solve problems, the author and family, like many others, don't plan to fly anywhere on January 1st, 2000.

But you're still on holiday enjoying your Christmas break. At 3 p.m. on January 1st, 2000, you decide to call your daughter in New York. However, remember that in this part of the USA it's still about 10am on December 31st, 1999.

An operating system is the lower-level software that enables your applications to work. Every computer must have an operating system. Examples include: *MS-DOS*, *Windows 95/98* and *NT*, *UNIX*, and *MVS*. Compare with application software below.

You use application software to carry out a specific task, like create a document. Common examples include Microsoft *Word*, *Excel* and *Access*. Compare with operating system above.

You talk about Christmas; the kids; how are they doing; How's Aunt Maud; the weather; what you're all doing for the summer holidays; and so forth, and generally have an enjoyable family reunion.

After all, trans-global phone charges are at their lowest level for years and your phone company, one of the many newcomers that emerged to break British Telecom's monopoly, have provided a special 'new millennium' deal for customers offering really competitive prices when using the new cheap videophones. It's Christmas you say and 'to hell with the cost!'

Photo courtesy of ProMedia Software

Fifteen, twenty-five, thirty-five minutes go by. You finally round off your conversation, say your goodbyes, break the com-link and log off after about 45 minutes.

You finish your second glass of *Chateauneuf-du-Pape* with a warm, satisfied glow: until the automated bill arrives two months later in which this one call is billed to have lasted 99 years!

Unlikely? Perhaps, but certainly possible. But who can *really* know? Perhaps the phone company's charges were so low because they hadn't really addressed the millennium bug properly. Don't phone your phone company to query the bill!

Widgets for value: high street chain

Imagine a well known chain of retail stores. They've established shops in most large towns and cities across the UK (or any other country). Let's pick one consumer product from the many thousands available with a shelf life of say 5 years – the exact product doesn't really matter.

BEWARE

DON'T MOVE THE DATE FORWARD ON YOUR COMPUTER SYSTEMS. This *can* cause damage: read all of chapter 16 – *Testing PC Hardware for the Y2K Bug* first.

The Buying department at Head Office are convinced that over the next few years, this product 'is going to be a moneyspinner'. So they arrange for batches of 5000 to be delivered to each of the 150 branches across the country in October 1998, ready for the Christmas season.

As the products arrive and are checked off at the branches, this information is electronically fed back to the central computer system, the 'old but *reliable*' X1000 (an imaginary name dreamed up by the author). The X1000 logs the product line in and calculates the shelf life to be 1998 + 5. If any of these items are still left on the shelves after the appropriate date in 2003, the marvels of modern computer wizardry will flag all the remaining items at all the stores and the company will simply send instructions to the branches to remove them. Fine so far!

REMEMBER

The most basic realisation echoed throughout this book is that there's no simple, single answer to the Year 2000 problem. Why? Simply because of the wide variety and complexity of computer systems and other electronic devices in use across the globe today.

But is it? This company didn't resolve the Year 2000 bug *properly*. The twenty-year-old computer system uses the two-digit format for handling the year information in the date. So the '03' in '2003' is not seen as 2003 by the X1000 system. As this configuration can't handle dates properly beyond 2000, the X1000 simply thinks the century must still be '19', so it sees the 2003 value as 1903.

But that's not the end of it: the X1000 thinks this batch of stock is therefore 95 years old (1998 minus 1903). With a five-year shelf life, it produces urgent reports showing the stock to be 90 years out-of-date!

It's unlikely that this kind of glaring error would be present itself in such a high-profile private enterprise-based organisation as the one described here. But the point is, it's possible, and repairing these kinds of errors *after* year 2000 will probably cost a great deal of money!

Introducing the Year 2000 Problem

Every day across the globe millions of computers perform billions of complex calculations, and yet the untreated effects of dealing with the simple change-over date to January 1st 2000 has the potential to cause immense damage to the lives of ordinary people everywhere. In this chapter, we introduce the important issues.

Chapter Two

The Year 2000 bomb

Here's the precise definition of a 'bug': a design error that causes a program to stop abnormally or produce an incorrect result.

Even if a computer was made after 1996, it doesn't necessarily follow that it will be Y2K compliant. Although most should be, do ask for concrete guarantees.

When purchasing new hardware and software, be careful. Get your seller to guarantee in writing that what you're buying is Year 2000 compliant. Even in 1998, some new PCs are being sold which are not Year 2000 compliant.

The Year 2000 bomb – a dramatic phrase, but it certainly gets attention. It has also been called a variety of other less dramatic names including: the millennium bug, the Century Challenge, Y2K bug and the more sober Year 2000 problem. But just what is the Year 2000 bomb, or whatever we prefer to call it?

The Y2K bug is a big problem that has a simple cause: dates, or rather date formats. The central issue is that many of today's computers – ie, most of those made before 1996 – use two digits to store the year information in the date. For example: a computer might store 20th of January 1994 in one of two main formats:

- 20-01-94 (standard UK format: day-month-year: 20/Jan/1994)

- 01-20-94 (standard US format: month-day-year: Jan/20/1994)

Even though most computer systems today allow us to enter the year in four digits, in older systems, often the '19' part was assumed and therefore usually hard-wired into computer 'date' processing chips.

Therefore, when we come to year 2000, following the example above, in the UK, we might enter 20-01-2000 for the 20th of January, 2000. However, in a non-compliant unrepaired computer system, the first two digits in the year information (20) would be discarded, and the default '19' would be re-inserted instead, resulting in 20-01-00, which at first glance appears to be correct.

But remember, an unrepaired computer system would see this as 20-01-1900 not 20-01-2000. So the computer would think the year is 1900 instead of 2000.

The Year 2000 problem may also be present in tens of thousands of electronic devices in the form of 'embedded systems software'. More about that later. A similar problem might be present in computer operating systems and application software as well. Consider the following:

...cont'd

> **REMEMBER**
> **We refer to a computer 'system' as** any computer or series (network) of computers, their associated operating system, and applications. A network of six PCs running under Windows 95/98 with Microsoft Office, can be considered as one system.

- For advanced product ordering applications, the result could be disastrous: the controlling (and often automatic) software might think there's 99 years of credit available or that bills are 99 years overdue

- Software might think stock levels are 99 years out-of-date and so automatically start ordering massive quantities

- Similar problems could cause any non-compliant inventory-based computer systems to behave erratically at best

- Project management applications could make vastly incorrect projections of time and resources

- Missile systems could become 'confused'

Five bombs for the price of one!

If we're feeling emotive, we talk about the 'Year 2000 bomb', but if we take a really close look, the Y2K problem could be found in any or all of five areas:

> **REMEMBER**
> **Detecting and repairing the Year 2000 problem is** easier in higher-level computer languages like 'C', COBOL and SmallTalk, and harder in limited support-type languages like Assembler, PL/1 and Forth.

- Computer hardware BIOS

- Computer operating systems

- Application software

- Computer-generated data

- Embedded logic (the code hard-wired into microprocessors and CPUs)

Source: The DTI's excellent Millennium Bug Campaign symbol

Year 2000: it's a leap year!

If a Year 2000-related problem suddenly appears on your computer systems, don't panic! The technical solutions have already been devised and are available. But you still need two things: knowledge about the issues and a plan to beat the bug. This and other similar books can help you in both of those areas.

The Web and the Internet can provide you with the most up-to-date news about the Year 2000 problem. Just enter the 'Y2K' or 'Year 2000 problem' into your favourite Internet search engines.

Another separate problem may also develop in some computers with the way in which some systems view year 2000, which is also a leap year. However, the BIOSes (see page 18) in PCs shouldn't be affected by this problem. And the good news is that to-date, the author is not aware of anyone finding a leap year problem in a PC's BIOS.

However, the leap year problem mentioned here could occur if a computer programmer had designed some code that doesn't meet the true leap year conditions. Let's examine these conditions a little closer. Certain rules are used to determine whether any particular year is a leap year as shown in the following question and answer steps:

1. Is the year divisible by 4? If it is, then it's a leap year, unless:

2. It's divisible by 100. If it is, then it's not a leap year, unless:

3. It's divisible by 400. Then it is a leap year

From the sequence above, it's clear that the year 1900 was not a leap year whereas the year 2000 will be. Many programmers developing software in the past were not aware of the true method of defining leap years, so there's a good chance that some software may not recognise 2000 as a leap year. So what, you may say!

If that happens, a computer system might think that February 29th, 2000 is March 1st, 2000. The question then arises as to what extent this error will have on say accounting-, forward ordering-, payment- and project planning-based systems, to name but a few. Also, some code that may appear to detect a leap year has been found to test only up to step 2 in the sequence above.

Examine closely all bespoke and off-the-shelf software and hardware if necessary. Crucial things to check: that February 29th, 2000 is a Tuesday; Wednesday March 1st, 2000 is a Wednesday, and the 366 days in the leap year.

Some current reactions

REMEMBER **You can test your PC for any potential leap year problems by carrying out the tests in Chapter 16 but using February 29, 2000 as the test date.**

REMEMBER **Every PC with a BIOS should automatically detect year 2000 as a leap year. Therefore, a leap year test for a PC is usually unnecessary.**

BEWARE **Get written guarantees of Y2K compliancy. Here's why: in 1997 a US Defence Department official purchased 30 Pentium-based 'Y2K-compliant' laptops. Of those, 12 failed when put through the date roll-over test.**

Globally, the Year 2000 problem could cause much damage and disruption if left untested and untreated. When we consider how much of modern life is dependent on electronic devices and computer systems, we can perhaps appreciate why the effect on the human population of widespread inadequate Y2K conversions has been compared to the Black Death plagues of the Middle Ages and even World War 2.

Yet it's remarkable how only relatively recently the real threat is being widely acknowledged as 'possibly serious'. It appears most of the large global organisations have now frantically begun to address the issue with urgent backing from sensible governments.

The issue is also 'hitting' the media almost daily now, even in the far corners of the globe. But many other smaller- to mid-sized operations still have not 'grasped the nettle' and realised the implications of ignoring the problem.

What some people are saying

Here are some of the more popular comments that have been cited. All of them are either wrong or are dangerous assumptions. The central question is 'can we afford to take the risk of ignoring the facts?'

- 'Microsoft or IBM will come up with a fix before the problem really hits us'

- 'It's a moneymaking scam from the computer industry, just looking for more ways to make us part with our money'

- 'My PC is working perfectly; I can enter dates of Year 2000 and beyond into my software and it all seems to work fine'

- 'It's all hype; newspapers like something new to write about'

- 'They [the Y2K repair industry] just want to make more money out of us'

...

...cont'd

HANDY TIP

In this book, we've also provided some added value by addressing related areas, like buying computer equipment, backing up and computer security. In the margins also, you'll find lots of handy hints and tips, and valuable advice, to ensure your copy remains a useful desktop resource even after 2000.

HANDY TIP

During the next few years, the millennium bug could make or break businesses and organisations, whatever their size. One way to help keep key computer staff is to ask those staff to sign a legally binding contract in return for an agreed loyalty bonus timed to cover you up to and beyond year 2000.

- 'If it's as serious as they say, why isn't the government forcing us to listen and do something about it?'

The government way

Most forward-thinking governments are now seriously addressing the millennium computer bug issue. But even after considering the potential seriousness of the problem, in most democratic nations, voters don't take kindly to what they may perceive to be bully-boy tactics: waving a big stick over an indifferent population doesn't win votes at election times.

Governments, therefore, tend to rely on continually providing information about the problem and using compelling methods to gain we the public's attention through the media.

Not taking any chances!

As an example of how seriously the problem is being taken in some areas, one well known airline is not taking any chances. Even *after* their systems have been 'repaired' and certified as Year 2000-bug-free, they have publicly admitted that they don't intend to operate any of their planes on January 1st, 2000.

The cynical amongst us might suggest this sort of stance has powerful marketing value, and indeed it does. However, such forthrightness is still to be admired. The real concern here, of course, is for the reliability of onboard computer systems (that are now present on almost every trans-global jet) in terms of the Year 2000 bug.

Yet manual overrides exist in every passenger-carrying aircraft and air crew will no doubt be especially alert, at least during the first few weeks of 2000. So perhaps we're falling victim to the popular myth of scaremongering. Yet it is the positive faith of human ingenuity and imagination that will resolve all the Y2K-related problems – eventually!

Why did the problem develop?

Many computer systems were defined in the 1970s and even 1960s. During those times, memory and computing capacity was much more expensive in real terms than they are today. Consequently, programmers who found ways of saving valuable capacity were highly respected and admired amongst peers and customers alike.

One popular way of making these types of savings was to abbreviate the year-date information from four digits to two – making an apparent memory saving of 50% (when the full date information is compared, the actual saving is really only 25% – but still a worthwhile saving in older systems). So the software would see 1971 as simply 71.

REMEMBER **The Year 2000 bug is a managerial problem *and* a technical problem. Without *active* 'hands-on' participation, solid support and motivational leadership from management, there's little chance of overcoming these problems in any organisation.**

Also during those times, it was generally taken for granted that the century information was going to be 19 and so this need only be entered once: usually, this was done simply by 'hard-wiring' the century value directly into the relevant electronic systems or silicon chips.

The logic and advantages of doing this were clear:

- It saved money; always a big factor for any product

- In date-dependent systems, it was obvious the century value was going to be 19, so why keep repeating it?

- Designers expected the software to be replaced or updated long before the century value would become a problem

Many of these early number-crunching software programs have been working perfectly adequately for years, so the argument went, 'Why change them?' Until, that is, people began to realise the serious impact of a date roll-over to the new century could have on a wide range of computer systems.

Programs containing date calculations may interpret any date value greater than 2000 as 19XX. So for example, the date 2002 in these 'unrepaired systems, might be interpreted as 1902, resulting in gross errors and rampant confusion at best!

Introducing the BIOS

The Year 2000 problem can be present in the two areas that make up any computer system: the hardware and software. Most smaller businesses run software using either PCs or Apple Mac computers (or a combination of both), so the effects on smaller businesses may be just as damaging – or worse – as those on larger organisations and institutions.

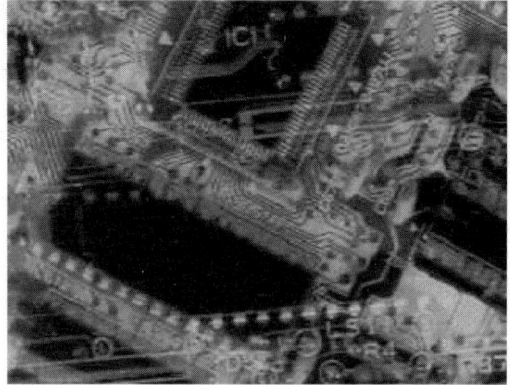

BEWARE

If the Real Time Clock is faulty, inaccurate, or itself contains a Year 2000-related bug, then the BIOS and operating system to which it is fed will also produce inaccurate dates.

The date information used by software applications is usually referenced to the date stored in the computer hardware. This date is referred to as the 'system date' and in most PCs it is stored in a silicon integrated circuit known as the BIOS chip. Precise timing is created by an extremely fast counter called the Real Time Clock (RTC), and it is this which is fed to the BIOS chip to control the date sequencing.

REMEMBER

In Read Only Memory (ROM) devices, stored information can be read but not written over.

REMEMBER

Think of the BIOS (software) as a kind of link or interface to the computer hardware (the electronic chips).

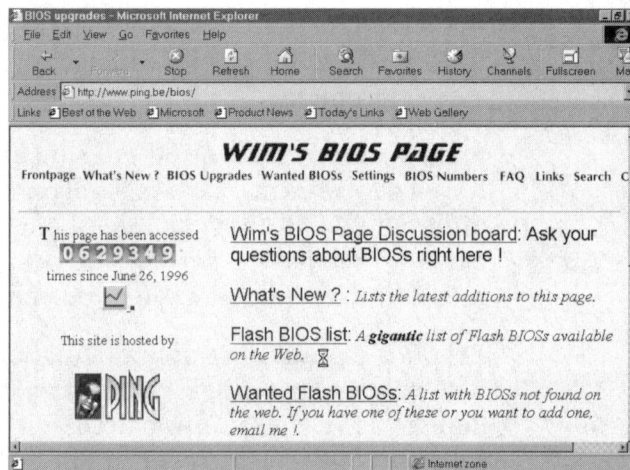

Check out Wim's BIOS page at http:// www.ping. be/bios/ for all sorts of relevant and useful information

...cont'd

BIOS is short for **B**asic **I**nput-**O**utput **S**ystem, and simply means this chip contains that part of a computer's operating system that handles communications between the computer and items connected to it. The BIOS information (often called ROM BIOS) is usually semi-permanent, so its status is maintained even when the PC is switched off.

HANDY TIP

To find out more about upgrading a PC, see *Upgrading your PC* **from the 'in easy steps' series.**

The most recent BIOS chips should recognise Year 2000 properly. But if you're thinking of buying a PC, you still need to be sure. Chapter 20 includes some *valuable* hints, tips and essential information you should be aware of when buying your computer hardware.

For existing computer systems, you can perform some simple tests to check whether the BIOS chip in your computer(s) will properly recognise year 2000. Chapter 16, shows you how, but CAUTION: do read the entire chapter *before* performing the tests.

BEWARE

Take care when changing a ßIOS chip: remember, computer components are susceptible to damage from static electricity present in your body. Learn how to upgrade your ßIOS before attempting it. Speak to your computer dealer or see the Handy tip above.

Some existing BIOS chips can also accept a software upgrade. These 'flash' BIOS chips avoid the need to physically change the chip. Seek advice from your motherboard manufacturer or computer dealer and check what level of compliance their upgrade delivers. Some may provide a respected label like Dell's NSTL (National Software Testing Laboratories) YMARK2000 test. Others may provide patch programs which, in the opinion of the providers, *should* deal with the Y2K problem properly.

See the NSTL Web site at: http://www.nstl.com/

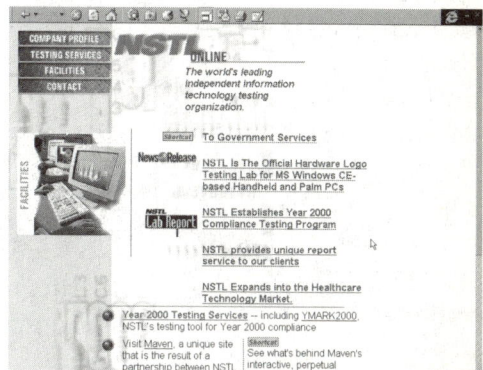

Don't fall for these five myths!

When considering the effects of the Y2K problem on software, the best result to hope for is that the program crashes. At least then you know for certain that it cannot handle year 2000 properly. Even if an application appears to work correctly, it may still contain Y2K-related faults. The only way to be sure is to check all hardware and software.

Computer systems most likely to be affected by the Y2K problem include those that can carry out forecasting, projecting, estimating and inventory control. Also, date-driven automatic stock reordering systems are particularly sensitive to the problem.

As we draw closer to year 2000, interest in the millennium issue throughout the media has increased greatly. A lot of theories and plenty of scaremongering has been put forward. But the plain truth is that we'll only know for sure what the general global implications of the Year 2000 problem are when we enter – soon – into the next century.

Nevertheless, let's try to rid ourselves of some of the popular myths about the Year 2000 problem:

- **Myth 1:** 'It shouldn't affect me should it? I paid a lot of money for this equipment!' *The cost of your equipment is unfortunately irrelevant.* The Year 2000 problem may still be present in your organisation

- **Myth 2:** 'Once I've corrected the bug in my hardware, I'm safe aren't I? *No, correcting hardware is only part of the solution.* Next, you need to address your operating systems, application software and data

- **Myth 3:** 'I've corrected all the hardware and software systems in my organisation, now I should be safe from Y2K-type problems, right? *Wrong. After repair, other people can 're-infect your repaired system.*

Also, if you receive date-related data like spreadsheets, databases, etc, from sources outside your company or organisation, and if this data contains Year 2000-type errors, you could 're-infect' your entire system with these errors (if you haven't put safeguards in place). You could also possibly pass the corrupted data onto others!

You need to address the issue of how your organisation deals with external data. *Step six: Staying alert* in Chapter 19, contains valuable guidelines to help you. Also remember, the Y2K problem may still be present in other electronic devices that may be crucial to your organisation – telephone systems for example: check these out too!

HANDY TIP

Here's one way to definitely beat the bug: assume the Year 2000 problem is present in *all* your computer systems, until the results of your tests prove otherwise.

REMEMBER

The Year 2000 bug could also be present in your Private Branch Exchange (PBX) telephone system. Contact the equipment vendors and ask for a written notice of compliance.

REMEMBER

You could also benefit by contacting your telephone line connection company and finding out about the Year 2000 status of their systems. As always, obtain written statements.

- **Myth 4:** 'My company is small; we don't have much software and only a few PCs, so we probably don't have much of a problem, right?' ***Wrong. Company size is irrelevant.*** One estimate suggests that even a small company may have up to about 2000 different programs, utilities, special routines and macros either running or available to run at short notice. Also, potentially the pressures are greater for small firms as there's usually fewer people, time and resources available to bring to bear on the problem

- **Myth 5:** 'We're a large, global company. We've got powerful resources and the best people so the problem shouldn't affect us much.' ***Wrong. Usually the larger the organisation, the worse the potential problem.*** Everything is so much more complicated in larger organisations. Usually there's a greater number and range of programs, utilities and macros in use and perhaps also a further range of complex variations to check, fix and certify as safe

Beating the bug step-by-step

No single individual, company or organisation that uses computers or electronic devices is automatically safe from any Year 2000-related problems. We need to:

1 Learn about the Y2K problem.

2 Identify how it affects us specifically.

3 Create a plan to fix it.

4 Repair/replace/update our systems.

This book is designed to cover all four steps. There's plenty of sound practical hints, tips and advice to address the first three steps. For step 4 above, we include some specific guidelines to consider as well as providing some key contact addresses and problem-solving sources to help. Alternatively, as Chapter 22 explores, you could take a revolutionary view and use the Y2K problem as an opportunity to completely re-invent your organisation!

Embedded systems software

We tend to think of software as being part of a computer system. But software is also used in many other electronic devices. In fact, anything containing microprocessors or sophisticated microchips could be affected by the Y2K problem.

These chips often contain embedded software – code that's permanently written into a silicon chip. The Year 2000 problem may therefore be present in these devices too. The following list includes some examples of the kinds of products which may have a problem with the year 2000:

BEWARE

Come January 1st, 2000, equipment containing non-compliant embedded software may (1) fail completely (2) fail partially (3) cause data damage.

REMEMBER

Microcode: a term to describe the low-level programming code that is 'hard-wired' into a CPU and which also controls it.

* Those computer modems and printers that use date information, and date-dependent office photocopiers

* Telephone and telephone exchanges

* Hole-in-the-wall bank terminals (ATMs)

* High-tech air conditioning in offices/plants

* Burglar alarms

* Traffic and train control systems

- Hospital CT scanners used in intensive care units and operating theatres for diagnosis of heart and other medical conditions. Even equipment used for sterilising surgical instruments is suspect!

- A wide range of other crucial hospital electronic medical equipment is also suspect

- Weapons, guided missile systems and aircraft onboard control systems (countries of particular concern include those of the Russian Federation and Eastern bloc, Israel, South Africa as well as Europe and the USA)

- Maybe some geostationary satellites too

- Some cars that employ computer controlled monitoring and control systems

- Some VCRs: setting the timer could be interesting!

| REMEMBER | **During your encounter with the Y2K problem, you may come across the term *firmware*. This can be applied to a piece of computer-type hardware but really refers to a permanent kind of software stored in Read Only Memory (ROM) format.** |

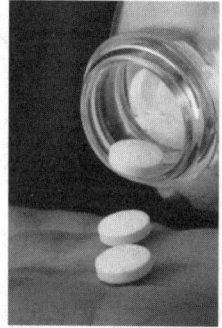

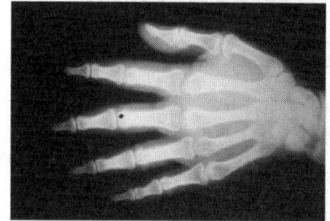

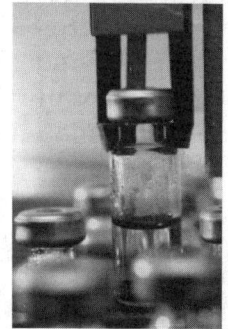

Providing fix strategies for these kinds of products is amazingly complex:

- Some products will have to simply be thrown away

- In others, the faults may not appear too serious and may involve a minor upgrade or chip change. But even this may simply not be cost effective: sometimes it's cheaper simply to buy a new item

- Any safety-critical devices may require a strictly governed 'serious' upgrade or complete replacement

Is it a computer virus?

The Year 2000 problem is not a computer virus in the truest sense, but we could be forgiven for thinking it is so. Here's a list of some similarities that the Year 2000 problem and a computer virus have in common.

The Year 2000 problem:

- Can be transferred between computer systems

- Can be extremely damaging to some computer systems

HANDY TIP

Although the Y2K bug is not a virus, from the data on this page you can see that Y2K problem does display some virus-type features. If you're having trouble convincing senior management about the implications of the Year 2000 problem, using a virus comparison could provide a powerful take-notice aid.

- Has a time-dependent trigger (00.01, January 1st, 2000). Some computer viruses are also triggered by a specific date

However, when we look a little deeper, we can see why the Y2K problem is simply a design failure and not a virus:

- The problem is fairly easy to detect

- It's present in all computer systems containing the design error (the Y2K problem). Viruses however infect randomly

- The Year 2000 problem can be present even on those computer systems that are protected against virus infection

- The Y2K problem was not designed to damage systems deliberately. Computer viruses are usually intentionally designed to cause havoc

- No antivirus software is available to cure the Year 2000 problem. It's just too varied, too complex and too huge for any single program to deal with

- It can be extremely damaging to computer systems but does not 'spread' using an agent. The only way the Year 2000 problem can 're-infect' another Year 2000-compliant system is if files from a non-compliant system are successfully reintroduced into a 'Y2K-cleaned' but *unprotected* system

Backing up Your Systems

If you use a computer, backing up your data regularly is an essential activity at any stage. When considering Year 2000 amendments, *before* carrying out any tests, checks or changes, it's especially important to back up everything on your PC. In this chapter, we examine the important aspects of backing up and data security, particularly from the Year 2000 standpoint.

Covers

Chapter Three

Why you can't afford to forget

BEWARE
For businesses, backing up is essential as the data concerned is often irreplaceable.

HANDY TIP
Always keep at least one backup copy of your data at an alternative location to the backup site.

BEWARE
A Configuration Management System (CMS), like a backup procedure, helps ensure the safety of your original data. However, do remember, as CMSs use dates to log software versions, so they too can suffer from Year 2000-related problems. Make sure the CMS you're using is Year 2000 compliant.

When you think about it, the chances are your data is worth more to you than your PC! A bold statement perhaps, but for anyone in business, data input is *always* going to be worth more than the hardware it's stored on. Lose your data and you could lose your business.

For individuals, maybe the risk of losing data may not have such dire consequences. But even so, these things are relative: don't and try and tell anyone who has lost a week's work that 'it could be worse'.

When we properly consider all the time and effort that goes into installing software, learning how to use it effectively, and then creating our masterpieces, we realise a lot of energy is usually involved. Sometimes, you can also spend many hours configuring your computer just the way you want it.

By backing up for a short while every day, you can safeguard all your efforts at a single stroke. So to those individuals charged with protecting computer systems, please, please, please back up at least your data *regularly* – especially those of you who have small businesses: you've more to lose than most.

In the context of the Year 2000-related problems, it's important to back up everything on your computer system. This includes:

- *The operating system*
- *All application software*
- *And of course your data*

Do this BEFORE making any Y2K-related changes or carrying out any of the tests outlined in this book.

The benefits of backing up regularly

HANDY TIP
To reduce the time needed to perform your backups, you could rearrange the data on your PC. For example: operating system on drive C and store all data on drive D. Also, you can choose to exclude certain file types like the *.TMP and *.BAK varieties.

HANDY TIP
If you're running out of hard drive space, as a quick-fix short-term solution, consider backing up non-essential files to tape or disk. Then delete the files you backed up from your hard drive. Do remember, however: there's no guarantee that the data on your backup copies will still be intact if or when you want to restore the backed up information to your computer(s).

Protect your data

If you use a computer in your work, ask yourself what the implications would be if you lost all your data tomorrow. Data stored in a PC can be damaged in many ways, including:

- Spikes in the mains electricity supply can cause data errors

- Lightning strikes can destroy a hard drive

- Hard drives can simply wear-out or crash

- Computer viruses can decimate a computer system

- And of course, remember PCs are stolen regularly

The only way to protect against these and other possible 'malicious' events is to backup your systems. Computers and peripherals can be replaced or covered by insurance if the worst happens; but all too often, computer configurations and associated data are personalised and unique.

Only you can ensure that all your hard work is maintained by ensuring your data is backed up regularly, or by performing an effective backup strategy yourself.

Overleaf you can learn about some simple but effective backup strategies. Once you get in the habit of backing up, the process becomes automatic – and may one day save your business as well as your sanity!

Establishing an effective strategy

Design a backup strategy that meets your specific needs. But make sure you make more than one copy of each data backup. For added protection, why not keep a simple written log of your backups.

You could simply back up your PC once a week to one disk or tape. But there are obvious gaps using this method which could potentially cause real problems if you needed to use your backups to recover your data. A better solution would be to use several tapes or disks. Larger organisations with extensive computer networks, usually have automatic sophisticated backup routines already in place.

Backing up using a disk-based strategy

For small businesses and individuals, an ideal solution is to use a disk-based backup solution. One popular choice is the Iomega Jaz drive. This allows backups to be carried out quickly and efficiently using 1Gb or 2Gb disk-based data cartridges.

Removable hard drive units (like the Jaz drive) can provide a fast data backup solution at a sustainable cost.

Iomega Jaz drive & Jaz disks. Ideal for backing up single PCs. Networked PCs can also be backed up using a drag-and-drop approach

To minimise the effects of any possible data loss, backup your computer systems regularly. Increase the backup frequency if you're working on especially sensitive data.

Jaz drives are available as an external desktop unit like the one shown above or as an internal add-on. The big advantage of using hard disk-based backup devices is speed: an entire hard drive can be backed up quickly. Data cartridges can also be password-protected to allow more control over who can actually restore or access the backed up data. Nevertheless, although tape-based systems always take longer, they have their own advantages (see opposite).

The Iomega Jaz approach is only one of a range of similar backup devices. You could also consider CD-ROM or magneto-optical backup strategies. Assess the benefits and drawbacks of all these systems with your computer dealer.

HANDY TIP **Even higher tape capacities** and faster data throughput is available using DAT backup tape drives. However, these are usually more expensive than Travan and QIC-based solutions.

BEWARE **Store backup tapes well away from** any possible magnetic sources, like telephones, loudspeakers, computer displays, and so on. The magnetic fields present in these devices can ruin a tape backup.

BEWARE **Before backing up, shut down the** programs you're not using: *Microsoft Windows* won't backup any open files.

Applying a tape-based backup solution

Tape-based backup systems have been used successfully for years as a popular method of backing up data on a Local Area Network (LAN), or to simply back up a single computer. Tape systems can offer a cost-effective backup solution that is ideal for Client–Server or Peer-based networks.

With a tape-based approach, it's important to establish a strategy that uses a series of tapes, so you always have a backed up system available if the need arises.

For example, let's assume you have a Seagate TapeStore 8000 tape drive, and your data content of about 2Mb is stored at one location. You could ensure a total backup of your data using two Travan TR4 4Mb tapes and four lower capacity QIC-WIDE tapes to cover the incremental backups.

The following procedure illustrates how such a system could work. The entire 2Mb of data could be backed up in under 1 hour and could run automatically 'in the background'. You could label each Travan TR4 tape FRIDAY 1 and FRIDAY 2. Next, label each of the four QIC-WIDE tapes, MONDAY, TUESDAY, WEDNESDAY, THURSDAY. Then carry out the procedure below:

1 Start the first backup on a Friday and back up the entire data content, using the FRIDAY 1 tape (see tip in margin of p27).

2 On Monday, use the tape labelled MONDAY to back up only those files which have changed since Friday.

3 Repeat step 2 above, using tapes TUESDAY, WEDNESDAY and THURSDAY each on their respective days.

4 On Friday, back up the entire data content again but using the tape labelled FRIDAY 2. This is the second full backup and completes the full cycle.

5 Repeat steps 2 to 4 to continue your backup procedure. Renew the tapes from time to time.

Backing up under Windows 95/98

REMEMBER

Before backing up your data, defragment the hard drive. Windows 95/98 comes with its own defragmenter tool accessible from the Start button.

REMEMBER

Keep at least one copy of your backup off-site to insure against things like fire, flood and theft to your 'office' backups.

REMEMBER

Before carrying out any Year 2000 tests or changes to your system, make sure you can successfully restore your backed up information.

If the data held on your computer system is crucial to your work or business, you should back up regularly. Ideally, back up the latest changes and additions once a day: this is your 'incremental' backup. Then, you could back up your entire system once a week. This approach is examined in the previous section. Alternatively, define your own system, but make sure it includes any backup 'gaps.'

A wide range of backup application software is available, but Windows 95/98 includes its own backup utility, Microsoft Backup. Microsoft Backup is an ideal general utility if you want to back up to the most common media, like floppy disks, hard drives (including both removable and networked drives) and tapes.

Performing a backup

Carry out the following steps to back up your systems using Microsoft Backup:

1 To start Microsoft Backup, click the Start button on the Taskbar followed by Programs > Accessories > System Tools > Backup.

2 Read any information that appears on your screen until you see Microsoft Backup in the Title bar. Choose the Backup tab.

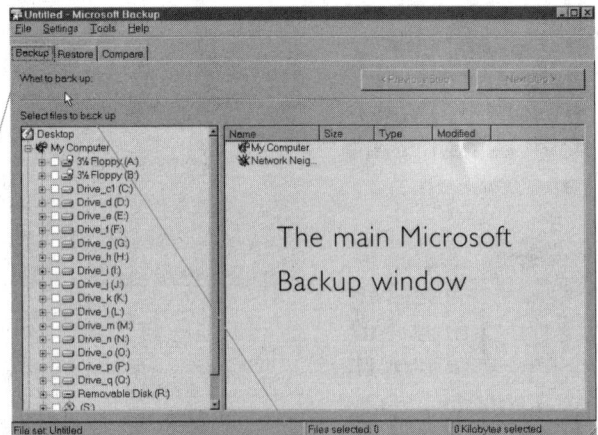

The main Microsoft Backup window

3 Open the File menu and choose Open File Set.

BEWARE

Back up your systems before carrying out any of the Year 2000-related activities mentioned in this book. This is your insurance against any unforeseen problems. Consider backing up as essential and not optional.

HANDY TIP

Windows 95 also includes updated versions of Arcada Backup agent and Cheyenne ARCServe agent for backing up to Windows NT Server and NetWare Servers. You can view more information by carrying out a search in Windows 95 Help (not Backup Help).

4 Choose Full System Backup.

5 Choose the Open button. Backup then takes a few minutes to prepare the Windows Registry and files. Windows displays the words Full System Backup in the Title bar.

6 Choose the Settings menu followed by the Options command.

7 In the Settings - Options window, click the Backup tab.

8 Choose the option 'Full Backup Of All Selected Files', then click 'OK'.

9 In the Microsoft Backup main window, click the Next Step button.

10 Click the destination where you want to backup your files.

11 Click the Start Backup. button.

12 Follow remaining onscreen instructions.

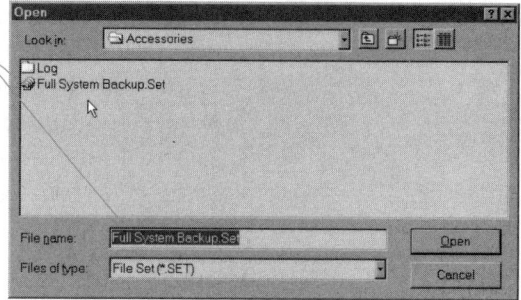

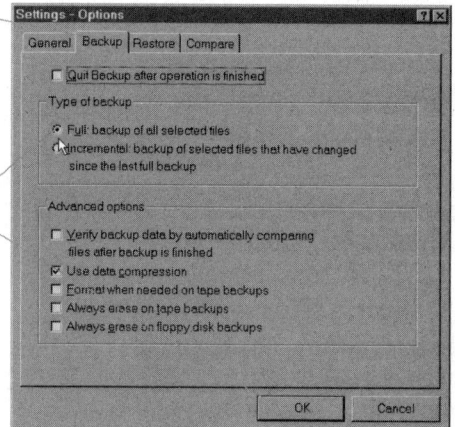

Installing Microsoft Backup

`You may need your Windows 95 CD-ROM or installation diskettes. Click Start>Settings>Control Panel, then double-click 'Add/Remove Programs'. Choose the Windows Setup tab and confirm that the Backup option is chosen under the Disk Tools category. Click OK and follow onscreen prompts.

Your application installation disks

Each software application usually comes with its own installation program. In Windows 95/98 for example, if you want to add a missing Windows option, you can easily do so using the Add/Remove Programs icon in the Control Panel. The essential point is, however, that you need your original installation CD-ROM or the appropriate diskettes.

When carrying out Year 2000 related tests, you can never be 100% sure what might happen until you've done it. You may encounter problems that might suggest the easiest and quickest way to resolve them would be to reinstall the application causing the problem. *That's why it's always better, if possible, to perform the tests outlined in Chapter 16 using an equivalent test system, not your day-to-day computer system.*

REMEMBER

Always keep your computer Start-up disk(s) handy. For example: during the install routine of Windows 95, you're prompted to create a Start-up disk, or you can create one from the Add/ Remove Programs icon in the Control Panel. A Start-up disk can be useful for starting your PC if problems occur which stop your PC from starting normally.

Consider the following guidelines before performing any Year 2000-related tests on your computer systems:

1 Have your operating system installation disks or CD-ROMs to hand.

2 If you use a network, make sure installation and setup disks or CD-ROMs are easily available.

3 Also, find all the disks or CD-ROMs for every application you have installed on your computer systems.

4 If you received user guides and other related documentation, it's a good idea to know these too are easily available.

5 Sometimes, we may install update patches and fixes. If you need to reinstall applications, you'll probably need to reinstall any follow-up patches or fixes also. Ideally, store these with the application disks to which they relate and make sure they have the correct version numbers and dates applied.

Identifying relevant file formats

Not all file formats are affected by the Year 2000 problem. It's useful, therefore, to know which file types are affected and which aren't. Although the following guidelines are aimed at PC users, if you use a different computer system you can adopt a similar approach to identify the 'hot' files.

REMEMBER An executable file is used to start an application. For example, Microsoft's WINWORD.EXE is used to start Microsoft Word.

1 If you haven't already done so, carry out an inventory of all your computer systems (see page 79 for guidelines). For smaller organisations you can do this manually, or software tools are available that can help you complete the task (ideal for larger concerns).

REMEMBER A filename extension is simply the last three letters of a filename. For example, in the filename CLIENT1.DBF, .DBF is the filename extension.

2 Examine the file directory structure on each PC and server. Establish and record all executable files present. These include those files containing the DOS filename extension of .EXE (for more information, see 'Remember' item in margin).

3 Also, examine the manuals that came with your applications to familiarise yourself with the different file types, especially executable- and data-type files.

4 Identify all the database and data storage-type files on your systems. Database files often use .DBF or .DB* as the filename extension (the asterisk (*) in .DB* represents any letter). Files with the extension .DAT are also often used in tape backup systems and usually contain data.

HANDY TIP In a DOS window, you can type DIR *.exe to see a list of all the executable files in the current folder or directory.

5 Identify which files are from commercial off-the-shelf applications like WordPerfect, Corel, and so forth, and those related to any bespoke software installed.

By default, Windows 95/98 stores documents in the MY DOCUMENTS directory. If you choose to store your data here, the chances are most of your word processed files, spreadsheets, database files, and so on, are listed in this one area, making the job of file location much easier.

File formats not affected by Y2K

Some computer file types are not affected by the Y2K bug. They are those that don't use date information. Those that do will automatically be fixed when you upgrade to a Year 2000-compliant application.

The second category listed above includes things like .DLL files. You'll often see Dynamic Link Library (.DLL) files listed in the Windows System directory as an 'application extension.' These files are used by executable programs (like EXCEL.EXE) that start applications. Although, an individual .DLL file may or may not contain date information, when its host application is upgraded, the relevant .DLL files should also be updated to match.

HANDY TIP

If your PC builds up a batch of unnecessary temporary files (.TMP), you can delete them to make more free space available. In Windows, first start the PC in DOS mode. Then, at the DOS prompt, navigate to the directory containing your temporary files. Usually, this is the TEMP subdirectory of your WINDOWS directory. Finally, type DEL *.tmp

Graphics files

We know pictures and other graphic objects can be stored electronically on a PC as a file. Common file formats include bitmap (.BMP), TIFF (.TIF), PCX (.PCX), GIF (.GIF) and JPEG (.JPG). If you're involved in contributing to a Web site, you may recognise the last two mentioned. Graphics files don't normally contain any date-related information. However, some graphics files may have a digital watermark applied to help lay claim to copyright. If such watermarks contain date information, you may have a problem: check with the relevant software vendor.

Temporary (.TMP) and Backup (.BAK) files

Windows uses temporary files for normal operation and .TMP files are not usually relevant to the Y2K problem. When an application shuts down *normally*, Windows should delete these files. However, if an application closes abnormally, then .TMP files may be left on your hard drive (see tip in margin). Backup data files (.BAK) are usually created by an application as a precaution against loss of the 'main' file, and are not essential for Y2K purposes.

Miscellaneous files

Other Windows-based file formats not relevant to the Y2K problem include: sound files (.WAV); files used in creating icons (.ICO); and information-type files (.INI).

Securing your data and systems

Computer theft is now big business. In Britain, it's estimated to be worth over £200 million a year – and still rising! Here are some ways to help keep your computer systems more secure:

- Don't think it'll never happen to you. Computers, memory chips, printers, Jaz drives, and so on, all have real value on the black market, and so attract a growing proportion of individuals who think the risks are worth taking

- Remember the value of your data *and* code – particularly if you've had bespoke software specially created. During the Y2K repair phase, your systems may be vulnerable to outside effects, even sabotage!

REMEMBER

During your Y2K repair phase, your systems can become particularly vulnerable. This topic is examined in more depth in *Assessing the new security risks* (page 81).

- Back up your data regularly ideally using two copies. Keep at least one copy of your regularly backed up data off-site at a secure location. Develop an effective backup strategy

- Run the latest virus protection software on your computer systems and keep them updated. Often, makers of reputable virus detection software make periodic updates available from their Web sites

- Log every piece of hardware and software: model numbers, serial numbers, software certificates and access numbers. If you haven't already done this, performing a systems inventory is a necessary step in becoming Year 2000 compliant anyway

- One way of reducing the possibility of being burgled is to try to avoid displaying that your have computer equipment present. If possible, move computer hardware away from windows and cover windows in doors to make visible identification difficult. Use blinds if they're available and even consider having tinted glass installed in key windows

- Have burglar alarms fitted to entry and exit doors and don't forget to cover emergency doors also

- Check the validity of everyone entering the building. Use closed circuit television systems and make them visible. Make maximum use of digital keypad access systems

- Take special precautions with computer equipment placed within publicly accessible areas

- Consider installing software utilities which render a hard drive useless unless the correct digital key is entered. Advertise this fact on the outer casing. Doing this will not stop a thief from stealing your PC, but it does immediately reduce the attractiveness of the booty and may make thieves think twice: they might decide there are easier pickings across the road!

- If thieves do get in, don't make it easy for them: consider bolting a PC to the desk. Fit internal PC alarms that activate when the casing is removed or that spray non-removable dye onto memory components if they're removed without authorisation

- Keep an audit trail of all software borrowed and lock software away when not in use

- Don't be afraid to challenge someone you don't know especially if they're behaving overconfidently or seem unusually overfamiliar: sometimes such an approach can be a thief's best method of deception

- Keep computer equipment present in cars covered or better still, don't leave any PC in a vehicle

- Avoid using a notebook PC case: carry your notebook PC in a brief case or other nondescript bag

- Invite staff to contribute ideas and reward those who suggest real workable solutions. Often the best ideas can come from those people who are working with the systems every day. Reward results!

- Review your computer security policy at least once a year and update it as necessary

Year 2000 Statistics and Viewpoints

This chapter is essentially about fear, denial, hype and desperate measures! We also look at why the practice of using two digits to store the year component of dates has continued until fairly recently. Then we take a close look at some of those amazing and shocking statistics! And to finish the chapter, we contrast the progress of smaller and larger organisations and consider the role governments can play in leading the way.

Covers

Chapter Four

What the experts are saying

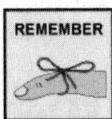

REMEMBER **Two main factors can contribute to an organisation's death come year 2000: (1) Year 2000 complacency and (2) starting too late to address Year 2000-related problems!**

BEWARE **It's been suggested that come 2000, some large government institutions like the British NHS or the DSS may develop hitherto unforeseen Y2K-related problems that may cause serious life-threatening events. It's clear that these massive complex organisations do need to pay special attention to prevent such occurrences.**

The year 2000 problem is not just about some computers' inability to handle dates beyond 1998 properly. From the kind of information provided in this book and other sources, we know the Year 2000 problem spans a range of issues, not just computer systems.

From concerns put forward on the Internet newsgroups, there also appears to be a risk that some key decision makers from larger organisations who are already hard pressed, may refuse to accept and deal with the Year 2000 problem simply because their retirement dates 'are imminent'.

Why the two-digit year format has continued

We know that the use of the two-digit year date format was common until fairly recently, essentially to create savings in memory and computing capacity. However, even though the cost of computer memory has, in real terms, fallen dramatically, the practice of programming in this way has continued until recently for a number of reasons:

- Only in the last few years has the millennium-date problem been widely acknowledged to present a serious problem

- If the two-digit year format was already being used in existing applications, the job of integrating new software with these applications was made much easier by simply following the same rules

- Changing two-digit year formats (DD/MM/**YY**) to four-digit year formats (DD/MM/**YYYY** or DD/MM/**CCYY**) is a complex and serious undertaking and requires a detailed strategy and thorough planning. Also, costs rise significantly: when bidding for software contracts, price is obviously an important consideration to everyone involved

Statistics: the Y2K guessing game

REMEMBER

For those countries planning to enter with the first wave into the European Monetary Union, the Y2K bug could not have come at a worse time. Many affected organisations are already struggling with preparing their computer systems for EMU. For these organisations, the need for in-depth planning, effective time management and imaginative solutions has never been greater.

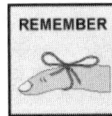

REMEMBER

Often, larger organisations contract many smaller companies. If these smaller concerns don't make their repairs in time, they may find their larger partners seeking alternative companies that have met the Year 2000 compliancy standard!

The Year 2000 problem is messy! It's not simply about just curing the problem; all sorts of other issues are involved as you can see in Chapter 11, *Legal aspects*. Generally, most experts agree that globally, repairing the Year 2000 problem is going to cost a lot of money. However, perhaps understandably, the estimates vary. Here's a brief list of some opinions and estimates already put forward:

- The Gartner Group has suggested the global bill could cost between £200–600 billion!

- J P Morgan have suggested the cost could amount to $200 billion

- A rather worrying statistic is that some banks and government bodies are still running software that is over 20–30 years old!

The software survival club

- Another estimate has suggested that the Y2K bug could make anything from 10 to 30 per cent of existing software useless unless rectified

- The Gartner Group has suggested that 90% of software applications will probably be affected by the Year 2000 problem, causing systems to 'crash' if the problem is not put right before 1999

Finding enough people with the right skills

- The Computer Services and Software Association have suggested there may be a shortfall of 30,000 computer staff by 2000, based on current trends

The United States

- The USA appears to bear the brunt of the Year 2000 problem in terms of cost: one estimate has put the cost of a fix at between $300–$500 billion

- In the USA, some estimates suggest that as many as 60 per cent of companies there will suffer Y2K-related problems come 2000. Of these, as many as 16 per cent are expected to cease trading as a result!

Britain

- Our Y2K problem is expected to cost in the region of tens of billions of pounds

- British Telecom have estimated their Year 2000 repair costs to be around £200 million

- The British Ministry of Defence put their estimate at £100 million

- Lloyds TSB estimate their Y2K repair problem may cost around £100 million to put right

- Recent estimates have suggested that between 40,000 and 'hundreds of thousands' of British firms may become casualties of the Y2K problem

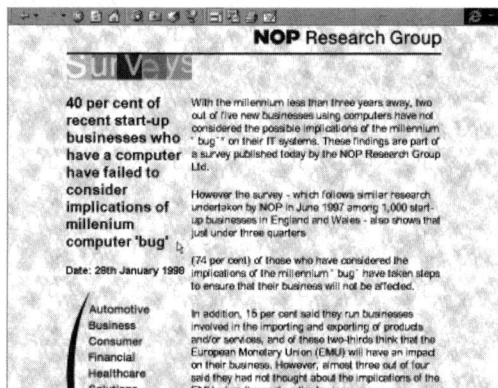

REMEMBER The way centuries are defined, can be useful in understanding the kinds of date-related problems computer systems can display. To recap, the 1st century stretched from AD1–100. The 20th century spans from 1901 to December 31st, 2000, so the 21st century will begin on January 1st, 2001.

REMEMBER With a millennium equal to 1000 years, the third millennium will start a few minutes after midnight on January 1st, 2001.

Repair plus litigation total costs

- From the expected litigation aspect, the Giga Information Group (US) are one of a group who've estimated that the 'ultimate' Year 2000 cost will be in the $1 trillion range!

Applying a little psychology

- Considering the size of the problem, the potentially disastrous implications and how so little time is left in which to create a fix, some people have been amazed at the slow response in addressing the problem. Perhaps our insulated, predictable way of life lures us into a false sense of belief in ourselves and that 'someone else will always find an answer'

Is it being taken seriously?

With so much media attention, the potential effects of the Year 2000 problem are being explored almost daily somewhere across the globe. Many of the world's more affluent governments have already set up significant consultation resources and have provided some aid investment. Unfortunately, some problems can be envisioned for the poorer nations and these problems may also spill over (like not getting paid) to those richer nations who are supplying goods and services.

Most of the reputable application software companies are taking the bug seriously: after all, it's in their interest to do so simply to stay in business come 2000. Often, Year 2000 repairs can be included in an upgrade. Customers are then more likely to feel justified in paying the cost of upgrading.

Larger organisations: aiming for smaller problems

Most larger organisations across the globe now know what's at stake: mere corporate survival. There's a scramble to address their own Year 2000 computing problems. Also, many of those organisations that utilise the skills and services of smaller concerns are insisting on 'statements of intention to comply', often accompanied by the threat of annulling contracts and working agreements.

Some smaller businesses heading for big trouble

At the time of writing, many smaller businesses don't appear to be taking the problem seriously enough. Some people even still think the Year 2000 problem is a computer mainframe 'glitch' and so need not worry. Businesses promoting this approach could be heading for extensive courtroom activity in year 2000.

Others think that the problem has been over-hyped by consulting organisations seeking to 'make a fast buck.' Some think the problem won't apply to them if they only use a PC occasionally or don't have computers on their premises. The truth is, the problem can affect anyone who uses electronic devices. How much people will be affected on an individual basis remains to be seen. Hold on tight, it's going to be a bumpy ride!

The British government's response

Britain's Taskforce 2000 – a government-funded body – was set up to address the Y2K problem. But to begin with, it appeared to achieve little impact.

But recently, a rethink has emerged. Tony Blair, the UK's Prime Minister, recently endorsed the seriousness of Year 2000 problem by making it a government top priority, with £17 million extra cash promised to help deal with the problem. This £17 million says two things: firstly, it's an acknowledgement of the seriousness of the problem. Secondly, it sends a message clearer than most other government bulletins that currently not enough money or resources are being employed to solve the Y2K problem.

Providing the Y2K issue is not ignored, the indicators are now looking more positive. By publicising the issues and now concentrating efforts on small- to mid-sized businesses and institutions, hopefully the casualty list in the first few months of 2000 can be kept low.

The 'embedded' problem again

Arguably, the Year 2000 problem present in tens of thousands of electronic devices across the globe could be potentially *more damaging* than the date-handling problems in computers! The bottom line is that nobody really knows for sure what will happen: the issues, variables, possibilities and ramifications are simply too complex.

Even if an organisation has been certified as Year 2000 compliant, there's always a risk that something somewhere has been forgotten. And that type of risk will always exist with this type of problem. Although human beings can perform amazing feats and sometimes win against almost impossible odds, the bottom line is people are fallible!

Perhaps that's why governments, the military, airline and banking industries, and the like, are looking for ways not to operate during the first few days in year 2000. And who can blame them!

The Effects of the Year 2000 Bug

Wouldn't it be nice to foresee what will happen to our lives in the first few weeks of year 2000? In this chapter we take an in-depth look from a computing aspect at who and what may be affected by the Y2K bug, and where and how. We also tackle some of the more essential questions you might ask.

Covers

Who is affected by the Y2K bug?

HANDY TIP

Some Microsoft products have Y2K-related bugs. You can easily find out about these in the Microsoft Knowledge (data) Base available on the Web or in CD format. To find out more, point your browser at: www. microsoft.com/kb/

BEWARE

We know the Y2K problem will affect non-compliant computer systems that perform calculations involving dates. Typical applications include: salaries, taxes, invoicing, interest on loan payments, credit card transactions, and any age-based calculations involving the current year.

The short answer is anyone; but some people are affected more than others. Those who work with computers are probably the first to feel the 'unrepaired' affects of the Y2K bug as problems here can become known well before 2000.

For companies and organisations, the Y2K problem essentially presents a series of managerial and technical hurdles to be overcome. Small firms who make up a supply chain to the larger organisations are particularly vulnerable. If any crucial member of the chain develops serious Y2K problems, the profitability of the remaining members can also be affected. In this scenario, it's easy to see how smaller firms who may not even use a computer could be ruined.

One disaster scenario put forward implies that many unrepaired computer systems across the globe will, from January 1st, 2000 either crash their programs or worse still, appear to work OK but *really* produce incorrect results, leaving businesses, banks and other financial bodies, to name but a few, paralysed and helpless. If this happened to any great extent, the financial markets would reflect the panic by wiping billions off share prices. At best, a global recession of the ferocity never seen before could result.

But this scenario does not take into account one of the most powerful tools we have available: the capacity of human beings to solve problems with ingenuity and imagination. It's this realisation that allows us to balance the viewpoint and examine a more optimistic scenario.

Who should get involved?

Within companies and organisations, the year 2000 problem is not just a technical hurdle; changes resulting from year 2000 compliance can affect the running of an entire organisation. Therefore, both managers and technical staff need to work together to create an effective solution, and one which, if implemented properly, can form the basis of a new, better system of carrying out an organisation's activities well into the next century.

What may be affected?

In a computer system, the four areas you need to be aware of are how your computers handle dates in (1) the ßIOS (2) the operating system (3) your application software (like Microsoft Office) (4) your data.

All aspects of computer hardware and software need to be assessed for Y2K compliancy, including computer networks and other hardware devices that are crucial to your activity (like telephone systems). Obvious hardware to check include desktop/portable PCs, workstations and servers. Software effects are discussed in more detail overleaf.

Come January 1st, 2000, there are two obvious possibilities for unrepaired Y2K-related computer systems:

- Some computer software will fail immediately. This is the best possible option for unrepaired software: at least then you'll know there's a problem and you can address it – even after year 2000

- Other software systems may continue to appear to work normally. On the surface, everything may seem fine. But the software may produce hidden errors which worsen the longer they're allowed to continue. This is the nightmare scenario and one which really must be avoided if at all possible

In most instances, a PC's operating system takes its date information from the PC's ßIOS. So in this event, even if the PC's operating system and application software are millennium compliant, if the ßIOS isn't, such a PC can't be considered Y2K-compliant.

Software applications can be affected by the Year 2000 bug in two main ways:

- Internal effects: date-related conflicts can occur in several ways – for example, at program inputs and outputs and during any processing, manipulation or comparison routines

- External effects: this is where a program interacts with others. A typical example is the common use nowadays of Electronic Data Interchange (EDI) in which information is passed electronically from one company or organisation to another

Software: a special attention area

Your software produces the results you want. Remember, there are two main kinds of software are installed on a computer:

The Microsoft Knowledge Base provides much advice about the Y2K problem. To view the current information, see: http://microsoft. com/kb/, then use the Microsoft search engine for the phrase: 'year 2000.'

- An operating system. Examples include: Windows 95/ 98, Windows NT (page 50), and MVS (still used in some large mainframe computers)

- And your application software. Examples here include: Microsoft Publisher, Lotus SmartSuite, CorelDRAW, and so on, plus any software that has been specially designed to meet your needs

Both of these categories should be checked for Year 2000 compliancy, along with your data. In the case of a non-compliant operating system or any particular application software, you may simply prefer to upgrade to the latest versions that are compliant.

Some software attaches special meanings to specific values. For example: the presences of 'OO' in the year could indicate an *unknown date* or *invalid record*. In other systems, 99 in the year field can mean *end of file* or *no expiry date*. This is why the Y2K problem could affect organisations as early as 1999.

One essential point to remember, is that when performing your tests on untested application software, try to run the tests over an extended period if possible – ideally several weeks. Why? Some software has shown itself to behave perfectly when January 1st, 2000 has been entered, but has then started performing incorrect date processing after just a few days of continued use. Take care, test thoroughly!

COREL WordPerfect Suite

Corel's **YEAR 2000** Policy

Bespoke software

Tailor-made software may present more of a challenge. Ideally, you'll need to contact the people who originally wrote the programs for you. If that's not possible, other repair organisations could possibly carry out the conversion. But do act quickly and remember, your data may also require attention. If your systems are complex, do discuss your options with a Y2K specialist.

What about MS-DOS & Windows?

HANDY TIP

Microsoft have set up the Year 2000 Resource Centre on the Web to address concerns from the public about their products. Go to: http://www. microsoft. com/ year2000/

REMEMBER

Microsoft have stated that the older version 2.0 of their Web browser, Internet Explorer is not Y2K-compliant. Version 3.XX and 4.XX appear to be compliant, 'with minor issues' still to be resolved.

HANDY TIP

Microsoft's MS-DOS operating system from version 4.0 and above should handle year 2000 dates properly. Earlier versions, however, definitely can't.

First, a definition. On their Web site, Microsoft use the words 'minor issues' to describe functions that don't interfere with the 'software's main purpose'. Therefore please note, we also carry that same definition in this book.

MS-DOS and Windows 3.XX

The only version of MS-DOS that Microsoft have stated can handle dates beyond year 2000 properly is version 6.22. And even this has some 'minor issues' to deal with relating to the Year 2000 problem. Microsoft has NOT yet warranted any version of Windows up to and including version 3.11 to be Year 2000 compliant. However, version 3.1 and above should not give any problems, providing the BIOS is compliant and working correctly: remember, Windows obtains the RTC value through the BIOS.

Windows 95/98

Tests performed on Windows 95 versions have provided better results. Windows 95 can handle year 2000 dates, but also has some 'minor issues' to be resolved. A fix for these may appear before year 2000. However, Microsoft have said that Windows 98 – which is expected to be available in Summer 1998 – will be fully Year 2000 compliant. For many, the simplest and probably cheapest Y2K solution might be to purchase and install the upgrade to Windows 98 when it becomes available.

But don't forget, although Windows 95/98 may be compliant, many applications which run perfectly OK under Windows 95/98 now may not be Year 2000 compliant. For example, it's unlikely that any version of WordPerfect – the well established word processing software – before version 7.0 is Y2K-compliant. Check your software with your vendor or view the relevant Web sites.

Some Non-compliant Microsoft applications

Also, Microsoft have stated that versions 4.0 to 4.3 of their Office Professional application suite have serious Y2K-related flaws and so can't be considered Year 2000 compliant. The same applies to Access v2.0 and Word for MS-DOS v5.0!

What about the Apple Macs?

Think different: that is the current Apple strapline often found in their marketing materials and on their stunning Web site (http://www.apple.com/). Where the Year 2000 problem is concerned, Apple have certainly done that and it's good news indeed! Here's why. The Apple Mac computers running the Mac operating system can correctly handle *all* dates up to February 6th, 2040 (or 2019 when using the *Date & Time* Control Panel).

Some of the localised versions of the Mac operating system often include additional features. For example: the Hebrew version supports the Jewish Calendar; the Persian version supports the Iranian national calendar and the Arabic version supports both the Arabic Astronomical lunar calendar and the Arabic Civil calendar.

But ...

Although the Apple Mac hardware and operating systems are Year 2000 compliant, you still need to check any other software installed. Some Apple Mac applications may not be compliant. And don't forget, things like Windows emulators and any Windows-based software you may have installed. If you're in doubt, check with your software vendor.

If the software you're using is not Year 2000 compliant, ask the maker what they intend to do about it and when an upgrade will be available. Ideally, you need to install this as soon as possible to ensure the new compliant software is compatible with any other applications you may use with it.

How will UNIX-based PCs cope?

If you use a UNIX-type operating system or software, you should contact your supplier, maintainer or system maker to determine whether your particular versions are Y2K-compliant and the level to which they're compliant.

Santa Cruz Operations makes the popular SCO variety of UNIX. The following paragraphs provide information about some versions of SCO software. However, new developments can occur quickly, therefore consider this information as a preliminary guide only. Also, it's always a good idea to verify key information from at least two different sources. The following flavours of UNIX (to-date) have not demonstrated any Y2K or leap year problems:

BEWARE

UNIX Classic software may not perform correctly after 1999. If you use UNIX Classic, check out your Y2K upgrade options with your supplier.

- SCO UNIX System V/386 Release 3.2

- SCO Development System Version 4.2

- SCO Open Desktop Development System Release 3.0

However, ALL versions of the following products are not warranted by SCO as Year 2000-Compliant:

- SCO UNIX System V/386 Release 3.2 up to and including version 4.2

- SCO UNIX System V/386 Release 3.2 Development System up to and including version 4.0

- SCO Open Desktop / Server products up to and including version 3.0

- SCO Open Desktop Development system products up to and including Release 2.0

- SCO Xenix 386 up to and including 2.3.4

- SCO Xenix 386 development systems up to and including 2.3.1

- SCO Xenix 286 up to and including 2.3.2

- SCO Xenix 286 development systems up to and including 2.2.1

Implications for Windows NT PCs

HANDY TIP **To see the latest information about any Year 2000-related problems with any versions of Windows NT, point your Web browser at the Microsoft Year 2000 Resource Centre on: http://www.microsoft.com/year2000/**

Come year 2000, some non-compliant PCs won't 'remember' the current date after they're switched off. The use of non-compliant software will only aggravate the problem. Therefore, for an NT-based computer system to be fully Year 2000 compliant, as with every other type of computer, the NT software, operating system used and hardware platform it runs on must all be compliant. Again, this rule applies to NT-based networks also (computer networks are examined in more depth on page 52).

So what about Microsoft Windows NT?

The Microsoft Windows NT operating system version 3.51 currently running many PC-based computer networks, is *not* Year 2000 compliant.

REMEMBER **The Microsoft NT 4.0 Service Pack 3 is available from: http://backoffice.microsoft.com/downtrial/moreinfo/nt4sp3.asp**

Anyone using this or any earlier versions of the NT operating system for business or other critical purposes should consider upgrading to Windows NT version 4.0 or the soon to be released version 5.0. Note: NT 4.0 is widely considered to be much more stable than previous versions.

Microsoft say the latest flavours of Windows NT Server and NT Workstation can handle dates of year 2000 and beyond properly, but with some 'minor issues' still to be resolved. If you're using NT 4.0, for the product to be labelled as 'compliant', Microsoft state you should also install the NT 4.0 Service Pack 3, and possibly one or two other related upgrades/service packs. For the latest information, go to the Microsoft Web address listed in the margin.

REMEMBER **Microsoft Server Site Express is available from: http://backoffice.microsoft.com/downtrial/moreinfo/siteserver3.asp**

Windows NT 5.0

Microsoft have stated that NT 5.0 will be fully Year 2000 compliant. Also version 5.0 promises to become Microsoft's flagship product of the next few years, aimed to eventually replace the Windows 98 operating system.

Computer Step expect to release an 'in easy steps' book covering this exciting product soon after Microsoft finalise their NT 5.0 offering, so keep checking the Web site from time to time (http://www.computerstep.com) or contact the (always) nice people at Computer Step to learn more.

Mainframes & proprietary systems

BEWARE **The Year 2000 problem has been described as a predominantly computer mainframe problem. This is wrong. The Y2K bug is almost certainly present in most older PC hardware, software, and electronic chips found in a wide variety of electronic devices.**

Many mainframe applications were originally set up to process the year using only two digits: 1971 for example, might be stored as 71. At the time, as memory and computing capacity was expensive, this approach was considered efficient. And as the century was obvious, this information – 19 in the previous example – was often 'hard-coded' into the electronic hardware.

However, if these types of applications are not updated to handle four-digit date formats properly, serious errors will almost certainly occur. For example, let's imagine a business involved in controlling large quantities of stock.

Inventory procedures for this type of business probably use Electronic Data Interchange (EDI) in which orders and payments for stock are carried out automatically using electronic systems, rather than the slower and arguably more error-prone paper-based routines.

BEWARE **A compliant mainframe can be corrupted by a PC used as a data entry front-end, if the PC is (1) non-compliant or (2) uses files that are time-stamped incorrectly. Remember also, the same thing can occur the other way round, with the mainframe being the culprit this time.**

One obvious implication for a non-compliant system like this is that the computer system may think that the current stock is obsolete and automatically order massive quantities of new stock.

Another high risk area is the financial sector. A bank, building society or other mortgage lender using a non-compliant system could make incorrect mortgage calculations, provide inaccurate age-related data, and so on. Implications such as these could be far reaching!

What action to take

To assess mainframes and proprietary computer systems for millennium compliance, consider the following guidelines:

1 As soon as possible, discuss your concerns with your vendor or the system maker.

2 And as always, get written guarantees of Year 2000 compliancy claims where you can.

The impact on computer networks

REMEMBER

Peripheral devices connected to your computers (eg, printers, modems, tape and disk backup systems), that don't rely on the date, should be Year 2000 compliant. But to be sure, always check with manufacturer or supplier. Many providers address these issues on their Web sites also.

REMEMBER

Even software drivers for peripheral devices like printers and modems, may need updating to the current versions come year 2000.

HANDY TIP

NetWare versions 3.12 and 4.XX are essentially Y2K-compliant (with patches applied).

If you use a computer network, dealing with the Year 2000 problem is going to be more complex than just dealing with a single PC, its operating system and application software.

To understand why a network requires special attention, first let's re-examine the relevant basic components.

What's a network?

A network is simply a collection of interconnected computers. A collection of physically interconnected computers is known as a Local Area Network (LAN). In a LAN, usually, there's at least one powerful PC known as the Server on which the central knowledge database is stored.

While on the subject of Servers, it's a good idea to have two Servers running concurrently: one then 'mirrors' the other, so if one server goes down, the other can take over.

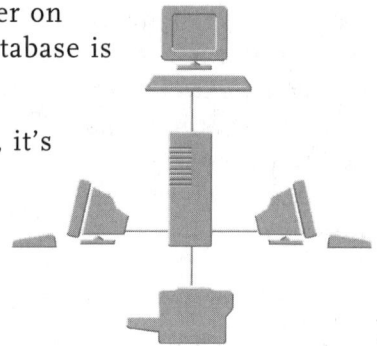

Other PCs or workstations (often called diskless PCs) store information to and access information from the Server.

The PC

To recap, remember in terms of the Y2K bug, we can think of a PC-based computer system as having three layers:

- The bottom layer is the BIOS or Basic Input-Output System; this information is stored in a chip which retains its settings even when the computer is switched off. The BIOS chip stores the date and time and information about the basic configuration of the PC

- The next layer above is the operating system and this 'sits' on top of the BIOS. Typical operating systems include Microsoft MS-DOS, Windows 95/98, NT v4.0/5.0 and UNIX Classic

Check your network infra-structure. If any routers, gateways, hubs or bridges use embedded-chip technology, then you may still have Y2K-related problems. Note model and serial numbers of the equipment concerned then contact the vendors. Cabling shouldn't give any problems.

Networks are vulnerable to date-type problems. For example, the server and workstations may not be date synchronised; incoming and outgoing email is usually time-stamped by the Mail Server, and this depends on its hardware clock (is it compliant?).

- The uppermost layer sitting on top of the operating system contains application software like Microsoft Word or Lotus SmartSuite

What to look for: the hot spots

Network server operating systems are one crucial area to examine for Y2K compliancy. Typical examples include: Novel NetWare, Microsoft Windows NT, UNIX, MVS, and PICK operating systems. Note: versions of Banyan VINES and StreetTalk should be Y2K-compliant, but always get written guarantees from your supplier.

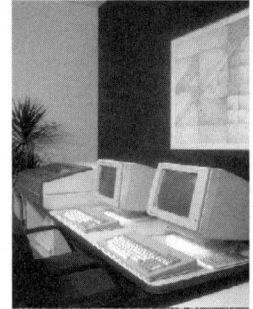

How to check a network for Y2K compliance

Considering the previous paragraphs, we can now put this into the context of a computer network. Here's what you need to do to check a networked system:

1 Check that the Server PC and its BIOS are Year 2000 compliant (perhaps check the maker's Web site).

2 Check the Server operating system is Year 2000 compliant. Typical Server operating systems include Windows NT, LAN Manager, NetWare and IntranetWare.

3 Check that *all* the Server application software is Year 2000 compliant. Remember, patches and updates may also be available from vendor's Web sites.

4 Check every PC and workstation in the network for Year 2000 compliance: this includes all BIOSes, all operating systems (like Windows NT) and all application software.

Minimising disruption

Throughout this book, we examine many different aspects of the Year 2000 problem, including strategy and technical solutions. However, one of the most serious side effects of the Y2K problem for most of the people involved is disruption – a simple word that packs a powerful punch!

Devising ways to minimise disruption

There are all sorts of ways in which you can minimise disruption. If you employ a consultant, consulting organisation, or Y2K repair body, early on in your project, discuss ways in which you can minimise interference to your day-to-day activities. Also, consider the following guidelines:

- Build in a 'disruption factor' into your overall action plan. Realise that disruption can be a real threat

- Those parts of non-compliant applications which interface with other applications often require some Y2K processing and will probably cause disruption. Research these interfaces in detail *before* implementing any changes to devise the most effective ways to limit disruption

- Use bridging programs where possible to 'buy' extra time and to help minimise disruption (see page 144 for more information about using bridging programs)

The impact of Electronic Data Interchange (EDI)

Many companies and organisations today use EDI to accept and send information. For example, EDI allows an organisation to send invoices to clients' accounts departments electronically using communications lines, rather than generate paper-based bills. Likewise, EDI allows payments also to be received electronically.

If your organisation is involved in EDI transaction processing, you need to establish with your Y2K advisors/repairers the impact and level of disruption to expect for data inflows (to you from your suppliers) as well as outflows (from you to your clients).

January 1st, 2000: everything OK?

Let's spend a little time examining what might happen to a non-compliant computer come year 2000. Here's what could be argued is a typical scenario. Although we relate mainly to the PC, you can apply similar effects to any computer system.

You switch on: the chances are everything will appear to run normally. But we don't want that: we want our PC to crash. That way, somebody who knows about these things would probably be called in to fix the problem. That's the best hope, because at least then we would know that we have a problem and can start to address it.

BEWARE **If you send data electronically to clients and suppliers, establish mechanisms to ensure you don't send old-style date formats by mistake to *any* of your contacts. Why? If any of these outside parties are not properly protected from 'bad' Y2K-related data, their data too would probably become 'corrupted.' Their lawyers will then probably blame you!**

However, what's more likely to happen is that our PC will appear to work normally. So we might conclude that all is well and so we too would continue to work normally. While we do that, the Year 2000 bug could be hard at work corrupting our data. Only we won't know about it. Or would we? We may not even realise there's a problem for days, weeks, or even months!

If that happened, what would we do? For sure, we would have to correct any non-compliant hardware and operating systems. Then we would have to update or replace relevant application software. If we replace our old software with new software, there's the often underestimated time needed to learn to use the new software effectively. Finally, we would probably have to go back and fix *all* the damaged data, backups included.

Remember also, under Microsoft Windows 95/98, basic printing functions are handled by the operating system. So if you print out your data, it's possible that the code used to, say, perform accountancy-type calculations is not the same code used to print the data. This can cause even more confusion.

All of this would probably have to be done while somehow still maintaining customer services. Quite a heavy load, even for the best organisations!

Broad implications: corporations

In any non-compliant computer system, any date information concealed in serial numbers may result in computational errors in which the causes may appear untraceable.

Here's another category of organisation that might be affected by the Year 2000 bug: those selling, organising and planning cruises and holidays.

If multiple software systems interact, changes made to one software system may affect the others. You need to identify any possible implications before making any changes.

Essentially, the Y2K bug has two possible effects:

- Internal, or from department to department, and...

- External exposure: your Y2K-compliant data may be re-infected through data received from outside organisations that you work closely with

Here's a more in-depth list of possible internal areas to check within larger organisations:

- Mainframes: hardware, operating system and code

- Mid-range computers: ditto to above

- Desktop PCs, Apple Macs

- Client/Server networks and other networks

- Portable computers

- All operating systems

- Programs and application software

- Queries, procedures, databases

- Screen displays

- Data, both archived and current

However, some software languages are more likely to be affected than others. For example, COBOL-based programs originally written in the 1960s and 70s and used in some large organisations, are prime candidates for storing the year information using two digits. And there's a surprising number still in operation today.

Then there's the question of whether any embedded software hard-wired into any of the thousands of electronic chips used in other devices may also contain the bug. If your organisation has expensive hardware that uses dates actively, contact your vendor to assess the implications in these areas. Then determine what the maker is doing about the problem and how this relates to your organisation.

Broad implications: small firms

Small firms, by definition, usually have fewer resources and less flexibility to deal with the Year 2000 problem than their larger counterparts. Therefore, as soon as possible:

- Determine whether you have a Year 2000 problem

- If the answer is yes, devise an appropriate strategy for dealing with it

- Establish exactly how the problem might affect your organisation

- Look into ways in which you can protect your code and data

Watch out for the not so obvious 'hot spot' dates. In any computer system that hasn't been certified as Year 2000 compliant, specific dates may trigger Y2K-related problems. For example, check the possible impact of any fiscal-related dates like the financial year-end, and so on.

BEWARE

But most importantly, don't assume that any Year 2000-related problems may be small ones simply because you may have a 'straightforward and simple computer system'.

Year 2000 problems experienced by small firms may not affect share prices or make television news, but problems are relative: a so-called small problem can devastate a small business if the wrong things happen at the wrong times. If, come year 2000, many small firms still find themselves with Y2K problems, then the trauma of their combined affects will also probably have a much wider impact.

A 'guilty until proven innocent' survival strategy

For anyone who uses a computer to create income, perhaps the best advice is to tell yourself firmly that you *do* have a serious Year 2000 problem that will end your business or terminate your employment in year 2000, *unless* you see demonstrable proof that this is not the case for every:

- Piece of hardware

- Operating system

- Copy of application software

- Disc containing previous software fixes and updates

- Other electronic devices crucial to your business (check for possible embedded software problems)

Broad implications: individuals

If an individual uses a computer system for private and personal use, then the implications for using a computer system on January 1st, 2000 are that it:

- Might appear to work normally but is still faulty

- Will crash – that is simply suddenly stop working, the mouse pointer may refuse to move and the keyboard keys might not work

- Behave erratically

- Work normally

HANDY TIP **If you use any Microsoft software applications and want to find out if your software will still work on January 1st, 2000, check out the Microsoft Year 2000 Resource Centre Web site at: http://www. microsoft.com/ year2000**

How seriously the Year 2000 problem affects you directly depends on what you use a computer for. Basic word processing, surfing the Internet and playing games probably won't cause you Year 2000-related problems. But if using a computer is an important part of your work, then the issue immediately becomes more important.

Using a computer for work or business

If you spend some time working from home (or 'on the road') using your computer and your work involves dates, then the Year 2000 problem will probably affect you to a varying degree. Looking on the bright side, if your computer, operating system and all software are Year 2000 compliant, then the affects of the Y2K bug might be minimal. Most of us are probably not that lucky and so have at least some components that are not Y2K compliant.

Consider the guidelines and information provided in this book to determine if you have a Year 2000 problem on your computer systems. Note the guidelines in chapter 16 to check your hardware.

If you're self-employed carrying out computer-related work for other parties, come year 2000, if you deliver or present non-compliant data to those parties, they may hold you responsible or legally liable. Therefore, do take care and learn about the issues and what could affect you.

Year 2000 Winners
and Losers

Chapter Six

Not everyone is unhappy about the year 2000 problem!
Some are enjoying an enhanced bank balance being paid to
fix it in companies and organisations across the globe.
Others – most definitely the larger group – are finding the
prospect costly and damaging even with less than two years
before the date becomes 'active'. In this chapter, we
examine these aspects and also establish which computer
users are not affected. Finally, we illustrate a simple way to
set the date on a PC.

Covers

Who gains?

Before January 1st, 2000

Before the big day, some parties are set to make huge gains:

- Year 2000 consultants and 'local' consultants

- Year 2000 repair organisations

- Year 2000 tool manufacturers and vendors

But we shouldn't forget that any organisation that becomes Y2K compliant will probably emerge leaner, fitter and better able to deal with the new challenges ahead. Also, come 2000, these enviable organisations will probably pick up extra business made available from those organisations which did not or chose not to address the Y2K issue properly.

After midnight on December 31st, 1999

Come January 1st, 2000, there's one group that stands to gain significantly:

- Lawyers!

  Here's a stunning and frightening statistic: some Y2K experts have suggested that litigation costs could outstrip Year 2000 repair costs by as much as 20 to 1

- And to a lesser extent, there will probably still be a demand for the best consultants, repair organisations and vendors for some time. There's bound to be individuals and organisations who thought they were clear of the Year 2000 problem, only to find in the first few weeks in January 2000 that problems still remain

However, any company, organisation or individual computer user who successfully beats the Year 2000 bug is an obvious gainer, in so much as they'll probably still be in business come Christmas 2000. In an IT sense, they'll also probably have a new, greater understanding of the strengths and weaknesses of their computer systems.

Who loses?

In one sense, everyone who has a Year 2000 computer problem loses, in all sorts of ways. Even with the benefits of becoming compliant clear, there's no getting away from the fact that the Y2K problem causes much disruption in organisations and costs a lot of money to fix. And all this is simply to stay in business come 2000!

Let's look at who could lose much come January, 2000. Consider the following list:

- The obvious one: anyone being sued over Year 2000-related issues

- Organisations who thought they were Y2K compliant but come year 2000 find they still have problems

- Anyone who relies on organisations that have the potential to be affected by the Year 2000 bug and which are not Year 2000 compliant come January 2000

Even if a large company or organisation professes to be Y2K compliant, it's still possible that their repairs may be inadequate, which could lead to serious litigation problems later. Smaller concerns that rely on one or two large organisations for most of their sales are therefore most vulnerable.

Employees take the fall

Some companies may go out of business as a result of Year 2000-related litigation or through poor Year 2000 preparation. Employees of those companies concerned are one obvious group who will probably suffer as a result.

The not so obvious losers

However, remember that all companies have suppliers and so the knock-on effects may radiate outwards to cause further trouble in the global economy. For example, it's not uncommon to find some smaller suppliers who may service only one or two larger companies or organisations. If their larger client ceases trading for whatever reason, such a move could devastate the smaller supplier's concerns.

If you're involved in a smaller organisation such as those mentioned here, perhaps these few years before year 2000, can provide a window of opportunity in which you can develop ways of generating new business from a wider client base, and so minimise any potential unknown year 2000 impact.

Who need not be concerned?

REMEMBER

If your computer's year prefix takes into account all four digits required (like 1999 or 2004), at all required levels, then your computer should be able to deal with Year 2000 dates properly. However, do check with your computer vendor to be sure.

REMEMBER

If you've recently purchased any costly equipment containing electronic devices that use dates, keep all receipts and associated purchase documentation. If the device appears not to be compliant, you could argue that it should have been at the time of sale.

The question of who need not be concerned is in some ways a little unfair. It's reasonable to say that if the Year 2000 problem had not been addressed at all, then modern life on our planet as we know it would probably end. In that event, a new dark age could emerge.

However, there's no need to start stockpiling. The good news is that the problem is now being addressed right across the globe. Massive amounts of resources and the combined skills of many experts are being brought to bear on the bug. Whether it's being done adequately however, only time will tell!

Not everyone who uses a computer may be directly affected by the year 2000 problem. For example, if you use a computer entirely for any of the following, you probably won't be affected directly:

- When playing computer-based games

- Accessing the Internet

- Performing simple word processing tasks

However remember, most people in the developed world use a wide variety of electronic devices. So there's a strong possibility that we may experience problems with some of these devices also..

If the VCR doesn't record our favourite television program on the correct day, OK we're going to be irritated, but it's hardly a life-threatening situation.

On the other hand, if while we're speeding along the motorway at 70 mph, perhaps eager to see friends and relatives, the microprocessor controlling our fuel supply and braking system starts behaving erratically then the situation takes on a much more serious tone.

Unlikely? Perhaps. But if you're concerned about this aspect, my advice is to contact the car makers and ask for a written guarantee of Year 2000 compliancy.

DOS-based PCs: resetting the date

On most PCs, you can set January 1st, 2000 manually, and the new setting will be 'remembered' until you change it. A small number of PCs won't allow this. If so, try these options: (1) you might be able to upgrade your BIOS using software (flash) on a disk or downloaded from the Web (2) upgrade /replace your BIOS chip, or (3) obtain a software patch.

If your PC will accept a flash BIOS upgrade, make sure you install the correct version. If the wrong type is installed, your PC may lock up and be unusable!

After December 31st, 1999, if you're still using a non-compliant PC, even though its date processing may be flawed, here are two possible options to consider.

Some non-compliant PCs will accept year 2000 dates entered manually

You may still be able to enter post-2000 dates manually on January 1st, 2000. Some PCs may 'remember' this new change and so you may only need perform steps 1–8 below once. If this works, your hardware may be able to calculate accurate dates: but remember, other components like the operating system and application software can still produce inaccurate dates if flawed.

PCs that can't remember the date

To make matters more confusing, come 2000 some PCs, may be unable to remember the current date once they're switched off! The 19th century-based dates would then normally apply instead. Each time you want to work with accurate dates, you may have to repeat the date-changing exercise shown in steps 1–7 below. And each time the PC is switched off, the latest date changes may be lost again. Come year 2000, for a known non-compliant PC, you could try performing the following procedure to find out if your PC can remember post-1999 dates:

1 If your PC is connected to a network, you need to isolate it from the network. However, don't do this until you've spoken to your network administrator: check first!

2 Next, you need to display the DOS prompt. If Windows has already started, choose the command to shut down and 'Restart in MS-DOS Mode'.

3 You should soon see the DOS prompt – C:\. This example assumes C: is the hard drive that loads your operating system when you first switch on – this is your boot drive. Otherwise, you'll see the letter of the drive you're booting up from.

4   At the keyboard, type DATE and press the ENTER key. Windows prompts you to enter a new date. Type the current date – eg, if you're using the UK date format, you could type 19-12-2001 for 19th December 2001 (if that is the current date); if you're using the US date format, you would type 12-19-2001. Then press the ENTER key again.

REMEMBER

If while performing these steps, your computer displays error messages and won't accept your entries, check your operating system documentation: you may be using the wrong syntax.

5   (Optional) To confirm that you've entered the new date correctly, type DATE again. Windows displays the date you entered. Press the ENTER key to reaccept your entry.

6   Next, type the word TIME then press the ENTER key. Type the current time – eg, if you're using the 24-hour time format, you might enter 21:48; if you're using the 12-hour format, you would type: 09:48.

7   (Optional) To confirm that you've entered the time value correctly, type TIME. Press the ENTER key to re-accept your values.

HANDY TIP

Patch fix programs mentioned in step 9 may also be referred to as Terminate and Stay Resident (TSR) programs. Shareware versions may also be available: discuss your options with your computer dealer.

8   If your PC has accepted the new date and time information, you're half way to success. Now, switch off the PC, wait about 20 seconds, then switch it back on. If the date you entered in steps 4–7 has been 'remembered' by your PC, congratulations: your PC hardware may be able to handle year 2000 dates. If not, go to step 9.

9   If the date you entered has been lost and replaced with January 4th, 1980 – the MS-DOS 'birthday date' – or some date other than the correct current date, then you have several options: (1) leave it as it is (2) update the BIOS by either using a flash (software diskette) upgrade or by replacing the chip (3) use a patch fix program (4) upgrade your motherboard (5) purchase another compliant computer.

Windows PCs: resetting the date

You can easily reset the date to the current date in Windows 95/98. Here's how:

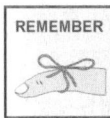

REMEMBER

If you leave your PC switched on just before midnight on December 31st, 1999, most PCs with the later versions of DOS and Windows installed (those that are Y2K-compliant) will automatically roll over to the new century without even reading the BIOS.

BEWARE

If correct date processing is essential to your activities, it stands to reason, not to rely on the information provided in this chapter. Much better to equip yourself with the latest Year 2000-compliant components.

3 Click Control Panel.

2 Click Settings.

1 Click the Start button.

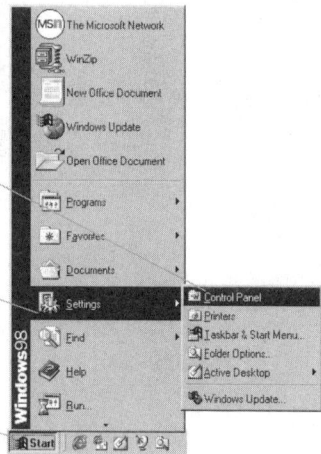

4 In the Control Panel, click the Date/Time icon.

5 In the Date category, choose the current year, month and day.

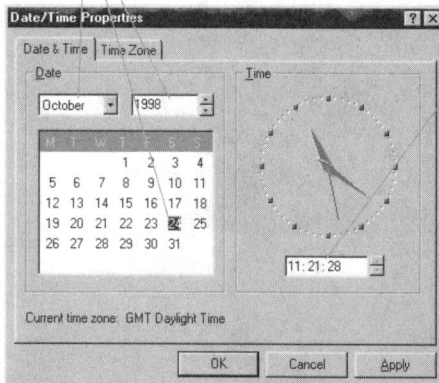

6 In the Time category, click to place a cursor in the box, then enter the correct time.

7 Click the Time Zone tab.

...cont'd

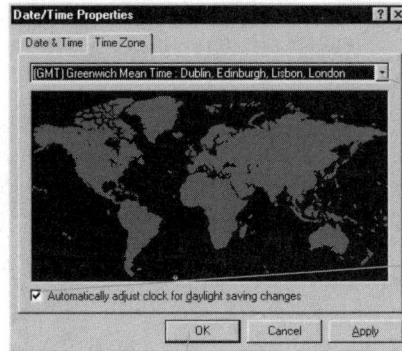

8 Choose the desired time zone: click the drop-down arrow box to see the list of available options.

9 If your time zone uses different times according to the season (like British Summer time), click here to place a tick mark in the box.

10 Click the OK button to confirm your changes.

Windows 95/98 also allows you to set the format for the date and time. Remember, people in the UK tend to prefer the DD/MM/CCYY (19/12/1955) format, whereas MM/DD/CCYY (12/19/1955) is preferred in the USA. To set the date format, perform the steps below:

1 Perform steps 1–3 on the previous page to display the Control Panel.

2 Select the Regional Settings icon.

3 Click the drop-down arrow button to display the list of options, then choose the desired region.

REMEMBER

In the Regional Settings Properties dialog box, you can also set the number and currency formats if desired.

4 Click the Time and Date tabs to see your format choices.

5 Click the OK button to confirm your choices.

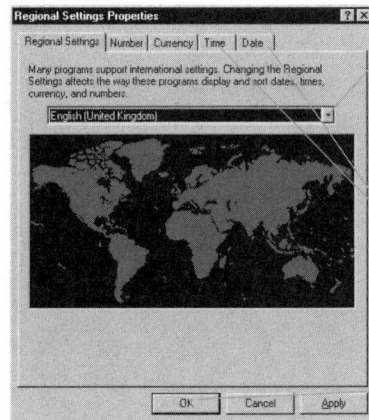

Countdown to Year Zero

'So what if there's a millennium bug, it's still at least a year away, isn't it! Plenty of time to sort it out.' We could be forgiven for thinking like that, but the truth is that Year 2000-related problems could *already* be affecting some computer systems if their problems haven't been addressed. Software forecasting is one example. The time to 'sort it out' is now; in six months it may be too late. This chapter gives you the facts and shows you how to establish when you may run into Year 2000-related problems.

Covers

Chapter Seven

Still plenty of time, isn't there?

No. Even though we're still in 1998, for many organisations, this doesn't provide much time to fix their Y2K problems. And remember, usually, the larger the organisation, the more complex the issues.

HANDY TIP

As we approach year 2000, time and resources may become scarce. Sometimes, you may not need an expensive upgrade. If a program patch meets the necessary conditions and fulfils your needs properly, why choose anything else?

Also remember, unrepaired software that performs forward date calculations may start being affected by the year 2000 problem as soon as 1999, or even earlier. For example, there's only one complete tax year before year 2000: April 1998 to March 1999.

Year 2000 repair prices: an ever-rising tide!

As we approach the end of the millennium, consulting and outsourcing resources available for dealing with the Y2K bug become scarcer and under ever greater pressures. Such events usually cause prices to rise and indeed this is what is happening today. The universal law of supply and demand is dictating the 'going price'. The demand for Y2K expert resources is generally expected to rise consistently in 1998 till peaking sometime in 1999.

BEWARE

Programs written in FORTRAN are more vulnerable than most to the Year 2000 problem. FORTRAN uses the value 99 as an end-of-file marker. Therefore, many unrepaired FORTRAN-based routines may start displaying errors early in 1999.

'Will the last person to leave please turn off the lights'

Companies and organisations that leave the Year 2000 issue at the bottom of their agenda may be threatening their own survival as the cost of providing a 'fix' may become so high as to be almost irrelevant.

Year 2000 experts able to provide the answers may soon be in a position to name their price!

However, sometimes alternatives exist: Chapter 22, *Thinking the Unthinkable: Starting Afresh* examines new ways of viewing the problem, even to the extent of following a back to basics approach.

When 2000 is really 1999?

It's possible for your computer systems to be affected by the bug well before year 2000. For some businesses, it's highly likely that they'll experience problems if their systems are not repaired soon enough. Here's why:

An application that handles only a few non-essential date calculations may be 'cured' by applying a quick patch program. The Time To Failure (as discussed overleaf) then can often be safely lengthened, allowing more resources to be made available for more urgent areas.

99999 for shutdown

One problem may affect some older 'unrepaired' computer systems well before year 2000. Previously, some programmers may have set up September 9th, 1999 to read as 99999 and this value-pattern in some computer systems means 'close down everything.' So software systems that use this method will almost certainly encounter problems if not repaired before that crucial date.

Many of the older non-compliant databases use '00' and '99' to purge or wipe a data record, or to start some other computational sequence.

How to create a record that can't be deleted

Here's the 99999 potential problem again. Many existing unrepaired databases also use the date pattern 9/9/99 to mean 'don't delete.' Therefore, if such a system reads a file containing the date September 9th, 1999, the chances are this file will under these circumstances never be deleted. In reality, a computer system could be processing tens of thousands of files containing this date – one possible result: utter confusion and system breakdown.

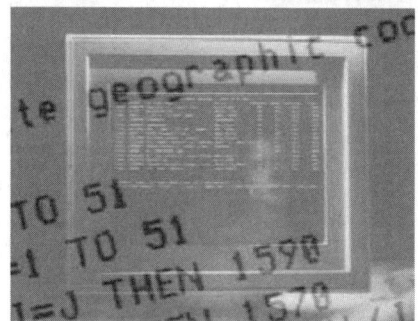

Establishing when you'll hit the wall

'When will we hit the wall?' – a phrase applied to mean when will the Y2K bug start to affect us, and a common question from many people wondering when the first effects of the year 2000 will be felt.

The Time To Failure (TTF)

We can use the phrase Time To Failure (TTF) to mean the date when an application will cease to handle dates properly due to the millennium bug. The TTF may vary from application to application and so for each non-compliant application, early on in the repair cycle, we need to establish TTFs for *all* relevant applications whether from internal or from external causes.

As we've seen earlier in this chapter, if you're involved in any kind of forward planning or forecasting several years ahead, you may have already come up against some strange effects – if you're lucky. If something happens to alert you to the fact, then at least you know about it and can do something to correct the problem. The real problems occur when there are no obvious effects. As a result, your financial calculations will probably be in error and you may not realise the errors for some time. If you're in business, the implications could be expensive.

How do we determine the TTF?

Here, there's no simple answer or solution; every organisation is different with different inputs. However, the most important point to realise is that the TTF is *not* necessarily January 1st, 2000. As we've seen elsewhere in this book, some applications – especially those that perform forward-date calculations – may fail sooner.

The type of date calculation carried out by an application can help determine its TTF. For example, let's imagine an application which deals with car insurance policies. Here, renewal dates are established 12 months in advance, so for a non-compliant system, in say August 1998, we can expect problems soon after August 1999 – four months sooner than January 2000, which doesn't allow much time for repair.

HANDY TIP

When establishing Time To Failure dates, try to build in a few months extra to allow for testing the repaired system in a 'live', working environment. That way, you won't get any nasty shocks if the results of the tests prove that some further repair work is necessary.

BEWARE

For computer systems that provide essential functions to an organisation, *thorough* testing is a vitally important activity that should not be curtailed or underestimated.

Devising a Fix Strategy

So far, we've examined the basics of the Year 2000 problem and we've looked at how soon it could affect us. Now we need to work out how to tackle the problem. This chapter examines several methods and approaches the important issue of liaising with clients and suppliers and how to treat the new security risks while dealing with the Year 2000 problem.

Covers

The cost of ignoring the problem

Today, many key business people lead extremely busy lives and are constrained to spend much of their day dealing with 'the important' day-to-day issues; after all, these aspects pay the invoices this month, next month, the month after, and so on.

During the busy working day, it's all too easy to simply ignore the Year 2000 issue. In some ways, the names we apply to the problem don't help: Year 2000 bug; millennium problem, and so on, all imply that the 'problem' won't necessarily become a problem for at least a couple of years. This approach is, as you would expect, not a good one.

As we learned in Chapter 7, the 'problem' is with usage now, even if we're not directly affected yet, but simply planning to avoid business disaster! As individual companies and organisations, we may not even have a Year 2000 problem, whereas our clients and suppliers may indeed have a problem.

And their ability to carry out their normal business functions can start to affect us: maybe essential goods won't be delivered on time, or invoices might be paid two or three months over the due date – or maybe even not at all!

So what are the implications of simply doing nothing? If you're in business, in a word: expensive. Whichever way you look at it, if we ignore the problem someone will have to spend time sorting it out eventually.

If you're involved in a small business, then that will probably involve you. The problem may appear far worse than you originally imagined. It's better to err on the side of caution and at least find out exactly what the implications are come January 1st, 2000.

And if we can help out clients and suppliers who may possibly experience far worse problems, that's got to be good for business and for all concerned, in the long run.

Is there a quick fix?

The answer to the burning question is that unfortunately there's no quick fix. Not Microsoft, IBM, the US government, or any other powerful body can offer a single one-step remedy. The wide variety and complexity of electronic systems currently in use today presents an enormous problem. Also, many systems are unique, presenting an even greater challenge and often demanding a tailor-made solution: usually the most expensive option.

However, we can determine those components which can go together to help devise a strategy for dealing with the problem. First we can assess the options – two are available:

- (1) Make your existing systems Y2K-compliant, or

- (2) Use the Year 2000 problem as a launchpad to start again – from scratch if necessary (this second option is examined in depth in Chapter 22, *Thinking the Unthinkable: Starting Afresh*

If you decide your best route is to repair your systems, here's a brief overview of what you'll probably need to consider:

- Establish what needs to be done; create plans covering each aspect: time, money, objectives, etc.

- Evaluate the legal implications

- Carry out a systems inventory and systems audit

- Establish the Time To Failure (TTF) and devise an action plan to beat it

- Evaluate the technical solutions: assess the benefits against the drawbacks

- Look for ways to minimise disruption to normal daily routines and processes. Brainstorm ideas with colleagues and the people who will be most affected

- Implement the changes and continually monitor progress through to completion

HANDY TIP

A program logic patch, has three clear benefits: (1) it can sometimes provide a permanent solution (2) it can provide a quick temporary solution (3) it can help 'buy time' when there's not much left before problems will occur.

REMEMBER

If an examination of your software application code doesn't reveal any two-digit year references, don't assume you don't have a Y2K problem. You still need to also check: hardware, firmware, operating systems, software compilers, data and tape backups.

What is the solution?

REMEMBER The implications for software embedded in hardware is examined in more depth in Chapter 2: *Embedded systems software.*

HANDY TIP Sometimes, it's easy to think the Y2K bug can be dealt with 'when there's time available'. Try to resist this approach. Consider the Year 2000 problem as a 'real' threat to your way of life. Allocate time, money and resources to beat the bug as soon as possible.

REMEMBER Essentially, beating the Y2K problem involves three main approaches: replace, renovate or retire. However, Chapter 19 lists a few more options for dealing with your software.

The Year 2000 bug may be broadly present in four main areas: hardware (embedded systems), operating systems, application software and data. However, the number and complexity of computer systems in operation today, means there's no 'standard' solution.

Compiling a compliance strategy: an overview

As each organisation has different Y2K conditions, it's important to define an individual plan of attack or strategy. One of the best ways to do this is to start by taking into account all of your existing computer systems, establish where the faulty areas are and then create an overall plan to fix the errors. Sounds easy doesn't it. But in reality, the issues can be amazingly complex: that's why the need for detailed planning, project and time management become so important.

Devising a more precise procedure

However, from a technical standpoint, here are some guidelines illustrating one way of approaching the problem:

1. If possible, use project management techniques to monitor and log your progress to make the best use of time available.

2. Identify and record the location of every single date value used in your computer code.

3. Determine the best way in which to correct each problem and to minimise day-to-day disruption.

4. Start to carry out the most important repairs that you expect to take the longest first, before completing the others

5. Validate and test each repair.

6. Make any necessary amendments and re-test until correct.

7. Thorough testing is vital. Test and re-test covering as many possibilities as are practicable.

The Microsoft approach

Microsoft, like most reputable companies, take the Year 2000 problem seriously. They recommend a series of procedures for addressing and dealing with the Y2K bug. These have been rewritten below for clarity while keeping to the essential recommendations:

1 For each PC-based application that can't handle dates of year 2000 and beyond properly, upgrade to a version that can.

2 Set up your computers to display all four digits of a year as the default date format. This way, users are made aware of any possible errors as soon as a date is entered.

HANDY TIP

Microsoft recommends that all PC software be upgraded to 1997 versions or later. Software created within the last two years should be millennium compliant. But don't assume this to be true every time: the only way to be sure is to check each and every software application.

3 Establish how the BIOSes on older computers will deal with the Y2K problem. Then make the appropriate changes.

4 Throughout your computer systems, convert all years stored as two digits to four digits. Then confirm each conversion is accurate and valid.

5 Set up a consistent date format using all four digits of a year to use when exchanging dates between internal and external organisations and other computer systems.

6 In key parts of your computer system, put in place business logic and procedures to ensure you stay alert for data errors or sources of corrupt data, both internally and externally.

7 Make sure any Help desk personnel are trained in Y2K transition procedures.

8 Upgrade relevant hardware and software to tap the new ease-of-use functions for handling dates into the new century.

9 Re-host systems with Year 2000 problems to provide a flexible foundation for the future.

The BSI Year 2000 guidelines

Some time ago the British Standards Institute (BSI) were deluged with enquiries from many people with concerns about the millennium issue and how it might affect them. In response to these concerns, the BSI have addressed the issue by providing essential guidelines.

HANDY TIP

To see the full version of the BSI Year 2000 guidelines, point your Web browser at http://www.bsi.org

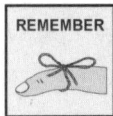

View the BSI's Web site at: http://www.bsi.org.uk/

They start by defining: *'Year 2000 conformity shall mean that neither performance nor functionality is affected by dates prior to, during and after year 2000.'*

The BSI have defined year 2000 compliance in four rules:

REMEMBER

Following the BSI guidelines will mean an end to the practice of attaching special meanings to specific date values. For example: 'OO' has been used to mean 'beginning of file' or 'not applicable', and '99' has indicated 'end of file' or 'no end value.'

- Rule 1: No value for the current date will cause any interruption in operation

- Rule 2: Date-based functionality must behave consistently for dates prior to, during and after year 2000

- Rule 3: In all interfaces and data storage, the century in any date must be specified either explicitly or by unambiguous algorithms or inferencing rules

- Rule 4: Year 2000 must be recognised as a leap year

The BSI rules provide an excellent benchmark against which to assess relevant products in your organisation for millennium compliancy.

Many other governments have also established similar guidelines to help their own people. However, as the Year 2000 problem presents similar challenges across the globe, arguably, most advice given will probably be broadly similar to that given by the British Standards Institute.

Checking hardware

HANDY TIP IBM provide useful background information about Year 2000 issues on their Web site. To find out more, point your browser at: *http://www. software.ibm. com/ year2000/ resource.html* Also, try: *http://www. s390.hosting. ibm.com/*

HANDY TIP If you want to learn more about computer networks and you like the approach used in this book try *Networking in easy steps* (details listed on inside back cover).

HANDY TIP Use the Web: PC makers often make available flash BIOS upgrades on their Web sites. This way, you can save money.

You can easily check desktop computer hardware for the presence of the year 2000 bug. For mainframes however, the issues are much more complex; talk to your vendor. For the more usual desktop computer equipment, carry out the tests outlined in Chapter 16. Remember to apply these tests to any Servers, PCs and workstations that contain BIOS chips.

Checking embedded systems

Here's a thought-provoking observation: On January 1st, 2000, there'll be an estimated 25 billion electronic chips at work across the globe. However, the good news is that of these, probably only 5% use date logic.

Embedded software code is 'hard-wired' into microprocessors and other specialised electronic chips. Sometimes, these microprocessors may be similar to those used in the mainstream desktop PCs.

Others are of a more dedicated nature, performing a fairly narrow range of operations. Also, electronic components may be used from a variety of different sources, so the precise behaviour – even amongst the same model – may vary.

Therefore, if any of these non-compliant devices use date information, come 2000, it's possible we might see different effects developing even on identical models. And in these circumstances, discussions with the supplier or maker should be your first priority, ideally well before 2000. Have model and serial numbers ready.

So many electronic devices could be affected, that there's no simple single solution (again!). The remedy may involve replacing a chip; a circuit board, or simply purchasing an entirely new replacement Year 2000-compliant unit.

If you're concerned about an electronic device that uses dates as an essential part of its function, you need to put your concerns to your dealer or the device manufacturer as soon as possible.

Who should be involved?

Management, IT and legal experts, employees, suppliers and clients make up the six main groups who should become involved with any Y2K-related problems in an organisation. Fundamentally, the Year 2000 bug is a managerial problem, not a technical problem. Technical solutions are available, proven and workable and from a technical standpoint aren't difficult, just time-consuming.

Perhaps the most pressing problem is lack of time. This is why in many organisations, two key groups will probably have to genuinely work together – often for the first time. Both managers and technical staff will solve the Year 2000 problem on local levels. But in some organisations, traditionally managers and technical staff have not always seen eye to eye. However, the Year 2000 project is one that must be delivered on time: this is one project that cannot be allowed to slip. In many organisations, basic business survival may be at stake.

REMEMBER

To estimate time needs accurately, managers need to get to know key facts about their computers systems. For example: the hardware used, languages, application software, and so on. This is why performing an inventory (outlined on the opposite page) is so important.

Devise a time plan

The nature of the Year 2000 problem is such that time – or lack of it – is probably the biggest hurdle to overcome. Managers can allocate the time and resources; technical people can provide estimates of the time required to repair the modules at each key stage.

But when time is short, looking at ways in which to manage time better is always a worthwhile exercise. One way to do this, is to break the problem down into sections; one of those key sections is time allocation. Then, establish an overall time plan. For example, estimate the time needed to perform essential activities like:

- Carrying out the required changes

- Testing the validity of those changes with test data

- Testing entire systems with real data

- Implementing the new repaired system and testing its operation

Carrying out an inventory

HANDY TIP

Here's a money-saver already realised by at least some readers. As a by-product of performing a systems inventory, you could find you've been over-estimating the numbers and so can reduce your insurance premiums.

HANDY TIP

When looking for instances of two-digit year dates, don't forget to seek out any documentation associated with your systems: it may save you a lot of time and money.

HANDY TIP

Software tools are available to speed up and help you perform a system inventory. Discuss your needs with several vendors.

Here's a startling observation: few companies or organisations know *exactly* which components make up their computer systems. To beat the Year 2000 problem, you need to know in detail all about your computer systems: hardware, operating systems, software, data types and so on. The best way to do this is to carry out an inventory. Performing a systems inventory at an early stage is one of the most essential stages of any successful Y2K repair project. The resulting information can also be useful in other ways (see Handy tip in margin). Consider the following steps:

1. If your computer systems are complex and numerous, consider talking to a Year 2000 consultant about advice on buying a software tool to help you inventory your systems.

2. If step 1 is not an option, then you need to perform your own inventory.

3. Start by thinking about your hardware: list all the different platforms (for example: PC is one, Apple Mac is another, Windows NT is another) that you have in operation.

4. Next, list all the operating systems you use (and any kept for stand-by/backup use) for example: MS-DOS, Windows NT, Apple Mac System 7, MVS, and so on.

5. Now determine each and every type of application software currently in use or stored for possible use. Obvious areas include: accounts, databases, spreadsheets, word processors, DTP, email, graphics, Internet, and so on.

6. Next, list any other remaining software; embedded, bespoke programs, utilities, patches, fixes, and so on.

7. Once you've completed your inventory, you can prioritise your systems and decide which are to be fixed and in which order.

Working with clients and suppliers

Contact all vendors and suppliers who provide goods and services to your organisation that are crucial to its survival and smooth running. You need written assurances that they too are ready for year 2000, or are addressing any Y2K-related problems.

If your organisation has Y2K-related problems, why not be up front about this with your customers. Let them know you're tackling the bug. Ask about their position on the matter too. Open communication has powerful reassurance value to all concerned.

In the context of the Year 2000 bug, we refer to suppliers as those organisations who provide goods and services to you. Sometimes, an important part of a plan for achieving Year 2000 compliance can involve any direct electronic links with suppliers and clients.

If you have electronic interaction with your suppliers – for example, automatic goods ordering using Electronic Data Interchange (EDI) – even if your systems are repaired, if one of your suppliers isn't properly Year 2000 compliant, your computer systems can become 're-infected' through automatic use of their 'bad' old-style date formats.

To make matters worse, when you send invoices to your clients, you can also infect their computer system with your now contaminated data.

If your organisation uses EDI or any other systems that involve electronic interaction, here are some important points to consider:

- Claiming to be millennium compliant is one thing; actually being able to demonstrate it is something else

- For your own protection, devise a method whereby you can confirm any Year 2000 compliancy claims your suppliers are making

- Discuss with your suppliers, setting up a 'standard' system to reject 'bad' date formats, so you all know exactly what is meant by 'bad date formats'

- In your discussions, consider what happens to rejected data. Why not try to establish protocols that ensure: (1) rejected data is automatically returned to the sender and, (2) includes a message attached to it so that the sender knows why the data has been rejected

- Ideally, agree other essential mutually compatible protocols with your suppliers and clients *during* the repair of your Year 2000 problem

Assessing the new security risks

HANDY TIP

To reduce the risk to your code and data while outside parties are working on it, always ensure the firm you use is reputable and think carefully before allowing any of your code or data to be taken off the premises.

BEWARE

Repair vendors sometimes offer to take your code and data and work on it at their own premises. This saves money, but you need to be assured that your data is kept safe, private and free from espionage! Choose a repair vendor with care.

REMEMBER

***Choosing repair vendors* in Chapter 17 examines these important issues in more depth.**

Many organisations will contract a consulting body to help deal with the Year 2000 problem. However, exposing any new people to your valuable and sometimes sensitive code and data, introduces new security risks. One key issue is how to find a reputable consultant in the first place. This aspect is examined in more depth in Chapter 17, *Choosing Y2K Consultants and Repairers*.

The purpose of this section is to simply spell out more clearly the security implications. Information, particularly commercial or organisational information, can be so valuable nowadays that it can be viewed as a kind of currency. If you're in business, you certainly wouldn't want your competitors 'down the road' to know your client list, your commercial advantages over them and details of your next earth-shattering product line!

Industrial espionage does occur even amongst some of the most unlikely prospects. Even though the risk is always present, you can still take steps to minimise any potential threat to your systems.

Be careful with tape backup systems

If you're involved in carrying out tape backups, even if you don't appear to have a Year 2000 problem anywhere else, the chances are that you do now. Here's why. Some tapes have a 'retain forever' date marker recorded on them. Many systems use December 31st, 1999 as the 'retain forever' date marker. The question then arises how the tape management system will handle December 31st, 1999.

After your systems are repaired, you still need to know what will happen on December 31st, 1999. If the system releases the relevant tapes by mistake so they can be overwritten, even if you manage to stop the action before the actual data is overwritten, the chances are the essential index reference will have already been erased – which means there's little chance of retrieving the original data.

The 'keep forever' status of this data may have strong legal implications. The best advice: know exactly what will happen to your tape systems on certain critical dates.

Establishing an outline repair plan

Carry out a systems inventory to get a list of all your current computer systems, both hardware and software. This information is necessary in order to carry out a systems audit as defined below.

Developing an effective strategy for dealing with the Y2K problem really means first establishing how the problem will affect you or your organisation: you need to determine the size of 'your' Y2K problem and the scope for dealing with it.

You could start by performing a complete inventory of all computer systems – both hardware and software – in your organisation, as outlined on page 79.

Here's a rough guide to help get started and establish what you need to do to beat the Year 2000 problem:

1. Become aware of the Y2K bug; learn all you can about it; read books like this one; view related information on the Internet and the Web.

The systems audit report should contain details relating the extent to which your organisation is affected by the Year 2000 problem. Contrast with systems inventory above.

2. Set up an interim budget; allocate financial resources to the problem; make a financial commitment – paying money is a wonderful way of gaining and keeping peoples' attention.

3. Perform an analysis to determine *all* the relevant present and future date-sensitive areas in your systems. Remember to consider how data from your suppliers will affect your systems and how data you may supply to your clients will affect them.

4. Now you can establish and agree a working budget and timetable for completion aiming to minimise disruption.

Like any complex project, make sure all your Year 2000 changes are thoroughly and clearly documented.

5. Fix your Y2K problems as discussed in Chapter 19: *How to Beat the Y2K Bug in Six Steps.*

6. Test and certify the validity of your repair methods; test its limits; spend as much time and resources as possible on testing; test over an extended period.

7. Stay alert! Keep your Year 2000 knowledge up-to-date. Application software manufacturers may issue periodic updates on their Web sites as we approach year 2000.

Updating Application Software and Data

The way in which dates are handled in software – embedded or otherwise – is at the heart of the Year 2000 problem. In this chapter, we tackle the issues that affect application software and bespoke programs and how to deal with one of your most valuable assets – your data.

Chapter Nine

Covers

From six- to eight-digit date format

BEWARE **Confusion over date formats could occur before year 2000, if you work with forward date processing and planning systems.**

HANDY TIP **It's usually worth discussing your outline options with several Y2K repair organisations. One may suggest an easier – yet just as effective – solution.**

BEWARE **Come 2000, six-digit dates like 12/19/01 can cause confusion. Even though we know the date refers to 2001, if you're exchanging date-dependent data with outside parties, your data will almost certainly cause confusion. This could result in legal damages being sought later.**

We know that the Year 2000 problem is fundamentally based on ambiguities caused by the different ways in which date information is process and stored.

The six-digit date format is at the heart of the problem but further problems are caused by the different ways in which dates are used across the world. Here are some examples:

- In the UK, most people like to use the day-month format: *DD/MM/YY* (eg, 19/12/55 as a short-cut for the 19th of December 1955)

- In the US and many other parts of the world, the month-day format is usually preferred: MM/DD/YY, (and following the example above, 12/19/55 is used to represent December 19th, 1955)

- And as many software systems are configurable, users can opt for the year-month-day format: *YY/MM/DD*, to represent 55/12/19 or 1955, December 19th

The problem with all of the above representations is that come year 2000, the two digits used to imply the year, will cause enormous confusion if not converted or repaired.

The ideal answer lies in moving to the eight-digit date format, which is simply:

- DD/MM/YYYY (you may see this as DD/MM/CCYY), so 19/12/1955 immediately becomes clear. The same approach can of course be applied whatever date order format you choose

To beat the Year 2000 bug, hardware and software applications ideally need to be converted or updated to the eight-digit date format.

Software conversion can use literal or apparent techniques. Literal means date conversion to the eight-digit format actually takes place. Using the 'apparent' approach, program logic implies conversion takes place. Either result is just as valid as the other.

...cont'd

Properly converting six-digit dates to eight-digit dates is usually the safer option – providing it's appropriate and is effective in every instance concerned. However, sometimes, true conversion isn't necessarily the best option, especially when dealing with archived data. For example:

- When there's not enough time to check large amounts of archived data

- Or when dealing with archived data that must be kept in its original form – or where legal repercussions might result if it's changed

HANDY TIP **When updating a software application containing only a few date processing errors, sometimes a program logic patch may be all that is required, instead of devising a full Y2K repair. Careful consideration here can save money.**

The important point is that such techniques are not usually available 'off the shelf', but often require a tailored solution. And with so much at stake, who wants to take such risks anyway?

Therefore, in discussions with your expert advisors, you need to identify from the options available which is the best route for *your* organisation. Often, a combination of techniques can offer the best overall solution in the time available.

Applying *Windowing* techniques

BEWARE **While repairing your Year 2000 problem, take measures to prevent your new systems from being re-infected from outside.**

Windowing has nothing to do with the Microsoft Windows operating system (or the see-though gaps in our houses). *Windowing* is a technique programmers could apply to the Y2K problem, by letting the software determine if the century information (the CC part of DD/MM/CCYY) is omitted or included.

For example, we could assume any two-digit year between 50 and 99 is a 20th century date (1950-1999), and any other two-digit number is a 21st century date (2000-2049).

If you use *Windowing* techniques to make a repair, different vendors may use slightly different protocols, so that it's possible the approach taken in your application may not work properly with your data. Check the validity of these methods before running on a 'live' system.

Dealing with application software

BEWARE

Bespoke forecasting and business planning software are two of the highest risk areas that could require urgent attention.

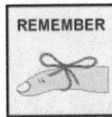

REMEMBER

Y2K repairers often estimate costs using 'Lines of Code' (LOC). LOC provides an idea of the size of an application, but doesn't allow for program complexity or other factors.

REMEMBER

Here's a typical example of an unlikely embedded software that may need attention: a computer used in a car to monitor fuel level/mixture, oil pressure, brake sensors and so on. It's possible that some of the chips won't recognise year 2000 properly and malfunction!

Commercial-off-the-shelf (COTS) packages

Application software and associated data combined present the bulk of the Year 2000 problem. A bewildering variety of non-compliant possibilities can exist. The only sure way to approach this problem is to check each instance one-by-one.

Contact the vendors of all your COTS software and ask whether their software is Year 2000 compliant. If the answer is no, you need to know how to make the software compliant. Ideally, discuss the wording of these letters with your Y2K legal advisors. Don't be put off. You want your software vendors to understand that you're not just another confused organisation. Of course keep all documentation you receive from them.

Bespoke software

Often organisations employ programmers to write software that fulfils precise needs, rather than relying on modifying COTS applications. Instances where this type of software uses dates should be considered as part of any Y2K-compliancy strategy. Remember, this includes not only the bespoke applications but also the existing and archived data.

Adopting a best value approach

To save costs, there may be a tendency to opt for quick-fix stopgap solutions: these should be avoided if possible as such approaches rarely cure the problems properly and may create larger problems later. One of the best ways to ensure all of this is achieved is to allocate enough of the three magic resources of any successful project:

- Time: difficult when the crucial dates are approaching fast

- Money: enough said!

- Planning: get the best people as soon as possible

Note: addressing the problem properly in the first instance is an activity that saves money in itself.

Checking and updating your data

REMEMBER **Even the embedded software stored in Microchips exists only to process its data. The data in these systems provide the real value of the product.**

BEWARE **Program interfaces – those areas in which your data enters and leaves your system – present the biggest problems to Y2K repairers: it's here that data is at most risk from corruption or re-infection.**

HANDY TIP **Compiling data in databases usually takes much effort. Here's one of the most important tips in the book: *try to ensure four digits are used in every instance to record the year status in databases at least.***

If we didn't have computer data, we probably wouldn't have a Year 2000 problem. Sounds simplistic doesn't it? But the point is that we endure the Year 2000 fix and all that goes with it, simply to protect the accuracy and reliability of our hard-earned data. Computer-based data can be classified into two main groups: archived and active. Archived data can be further subdivided into:

- Active data: that which you allow to be changed/ updated as necessary

- Data which, for whatever reason, cannot and must not be changed in any way

Active data is that which you're working on or data that is accessed regularly throughout the day. Also remember, once you change application software to handle new millennium dates properly, this change may affect whether you can still access your 'old' data. 'Standard' software that has been updated may not be able to handle 'old style' date formats.

Computer data can be found in four main areas:

- Internal interfaces (where data comes into a computer system from some outside source – eg, an order acknowledgement from a supplier)

- In a database (even a spreadsheet is a kind of database)

- As an archived file (like a word processed document)

- External interfaces (where data goes to just before it leaves a computer system – eg, as an invoice sent electronically to a client)

Secure your data in four steps

Whatever fix method you choose to implement, it should ensure four things work together to protect your data:

- (1) Repair the systems to ensure data integrity, accuracy and reliability is maintained

HANDY TIP

If your system encounters non-compatible date formats, two possibles emerge: (1) bounce the data back to the source and with a message saying why; (2) drop the data into the 'bit bucket', with no warning message to the sender (risky).

REMEMBER

Here's the common 'rule of thumb' often used to establish who defines the format of the data interfaces: the sender conforms to the receiver's format.

BEWARE

Devise ways to check all incoming data, especially data received from friends, colleagues and business contacts, to help prevent re-infection.

- (2) Ensure all information stores, such as current and archived databases, are processed and converted properly

- (3) Ensure that any data, new or old is not corrupted internally

- (4) Ensure that data is not corrupted from outside

Common repair methodologies

Currently, two common approaches are used to repair non-Y2K-compliant data:

(A) Convert *all* instances containing two-digit years to four-digit years (eg, 19/12/**55** becomes 19/12/**1955**). Then update the application and/or bespoke software to ensure it too creates all new data in the new format. Consider three points about this approach:

- It ensures the fastest processing time for your data

- It's also usually the most expensive method to apply

- Converting large amounts of archived data is costly

(B) Alternatively, leave the data alone and change the program software so that it carries out the date conversions within the program code. Consider the following points concerning this approach:

- Processing takes longer than (A) above

- This method is usually quicker, therefore cheaper than (A) above

- For any computer system using batch processing, this approach is usually ideal

- However, thorough testing is required to try to allow for all the possible combinations

In practice, a combination of the above methods is often applied to provide a working solution or to create more time to provide a more permanent fix.

How Much Will it all Cost?

'How much are we talking about?' No doubt this phrase, or its equivalent, is being repeated by many people in many different organisations across the globe, when confronted with the cost of defusing the Year 2000 time bomb. In this chapter, we provide a framework to help you estimate repair costs for your own organisation.

Covers

Chapter Ten

Defining cost by category

Estimating the cost of repairing the Year 2000 problem is not as straightforward as we might at first think. Costs can result from all sorts of different things. For any individual organisation, consider:

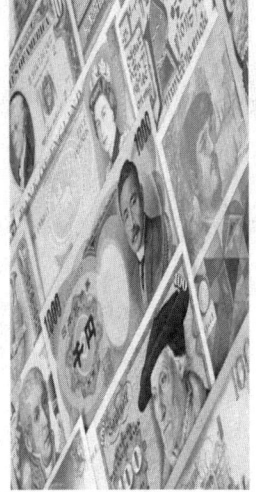

- The cost associated with doing nothing about the Y2K bug

- Direct repair costs: consultants fees, the purchasing of new software tools, hiring extra highly qualified and increasingly more expensive IT staff, and so on

- Indirect repair costs. For example: disruption, the impact on employees, equipment, time, and so on, and the effect on normal activities while Year 2000 repairs are ongoing

- Costs associated with litigation if things don't go according to plan

Setting up a Year 2000 budget

The diagram below illustrates the main inputs that can help determine a true Year 2000 budget:

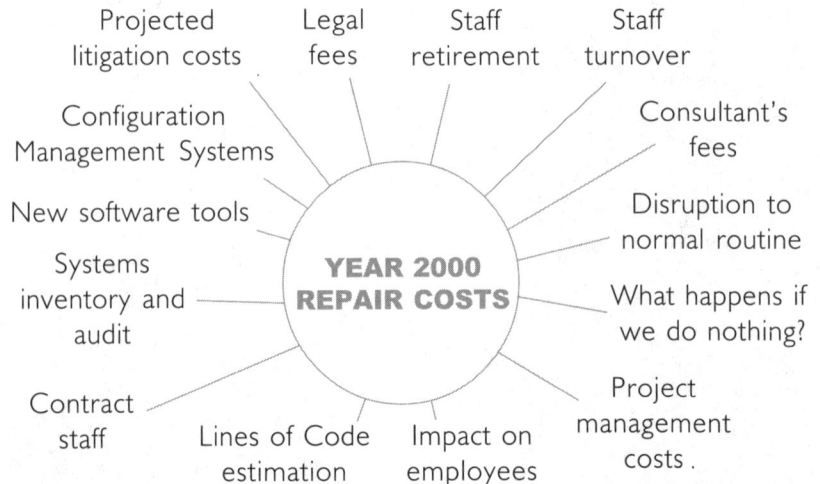

Projected litigation costs   Legal fees   Staff retirement   Staff turnover

Configuration Management Systems

Consultant's fees

New software tools

Disruption to normal routine

Systems inventory and audit

YEAR 2000 REPAIR COSTS

What happens if we do nothing?

Contract staff

Project management costs.

Lines of Code estimation   Impact on employees

Estimating Year 2000 repair costs

© Picture courtesy of ProMedia Software

REMEMBER

Each LOC is usually costed at the 'going rate' for the country you live in. However, as we near year 2000, it's conceivable that these rates will increase, perhaps dramatically.

Estimating Year 2000 repair costs is a tricky business; the variables are complex and no two organisations are the same. To estimate realistically, we need a standard unit of measurement – the use of the measurement Lines Of Code (LOC) certainly helps. We can then define how many LOCs need to be repaired and the rate for each LOC. And of course, every country has its own LOC rate.

What influences the cost of repair?

Remember, the LOC measurement provides only a rough estimation of repair costs. Other factors also affect costs. Consider the following points:

HANDY TIP

To find out more information about Lines Of Code, try pointing your Web browser at The MITRE Corporation Web site at address: http://www.mitre. org/research/y2k

- More often than not, the actual number of LOCs repaired will probably be higher than you might expect. Once programmers start the job of repairing your systems, they may find further LOCs need to be tested and the relevant code can be scattered throughout the system, not just in the obvious places

- Key IT staff may leave the organisation or retire. Keeping key staff loyal becomes crucial as we approach year 2000. Chapter 18, *Year 2000 People Aspects* examines some ways to help you bring out the best in your employees

- Even when estimating costs, if the Time To Failure is expected to occur before an organisation has completed Year 2000 repairs, some organisations may need to build in a figure to allow for possible litigation later. Year 2000 litigation aspects are understandably complex and for this reason are covered in more depth in Chapter 11

Establishing outline repair costs

Here's one way to estimate the cost of repairing the Y2K problem within any organisation:

1. Complete an inventory of all your computer systems: find out things like how many systems you have, which computer languages are used and the number of Lines Of Code (LOC) for each language.

Another valuable source of Y2K information can be found on the Software Productivity Research (SPR) Web site at address: http://www.spr.com Click on the Resources button, then 'Articles and News' to see information from the respected Y2K expert, Capers Jones.

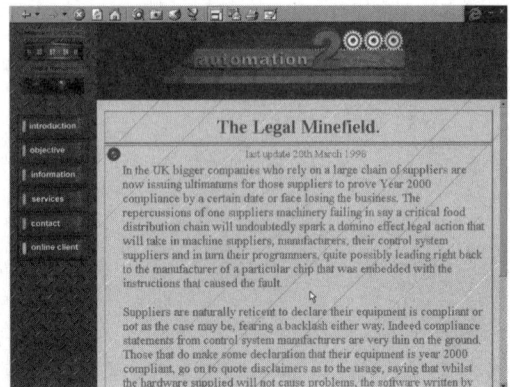

2. For each type of system, find out the rate for repairing a LOC. Next, multiply this figure by the total number of LOCs in that system. Then, add together all the LOC estimates for all your systems. *Eg, let's imagine each LOC costs the imaginary figure of £1, and we have 50,000 Lines Of Code, which gives us an estimated repair cost of £50,000 for this one system. We have three other types of systems each costing £25,000, £12,000 and £21,000. So our total thus far is £108,000.*

3. Next, we should include a cost for such things as business disruption, new equipment required, the impact of increased staff turnover, and so on. Each organisation should assess their own needs for this step.

4. Finally, we could build in an 'unknown' factor, to cover for such things as the cost of any possible litigation later, and for any remaining probabilities not yet covered.

Legal Aspects

One thing is for certain: the Year 2000 problem presents many challenges for businesses, organisations and individuals – some minor, some crucial. An important area to consider is the legal implications connected with all sorts of 'what if ...' questions. In this chapter, we outline the legal side of the Year 2000 problem.

Covers

Chapter Eleven

Legal implications: who and why?

The massive scope of the Year 2000 problem, and the short time frame available to deal with it, means legal implications can become crucially important.

REMEMBER

Larger client organis-ations may ask you to make a 'Statement of intention to comply'. And they may also ask you to record your current Y2K position and what remedial action you intend to make to ensure Y2K compliancy. If you make a statement, be careful what you say and how you word it: legal implications could come back to haunt you later.

REMEMBER

The law sees three main ways in which loss can be experienced in relation to the Year 2000 problem: direct, indirect and consequential loss.

National and international legal implications

This chapter relates mainly to English law and should be considered as a general guide only. Later developments may make some of this information redundant. Readers in countries other than the UK could benefit by trying to determine the relevance of any particular recent developments and implications specific to their country.

Also, we should remember that wherever we may live, the world is becoming ever more a global economy, so legal ramifications may become blurred and could extend well beyond our own borders. In any event, you should always take advice from legal experts experienced in IT law and who are knowledgeable about Y2K-related issues. Now let's look at the two most important potential legal implications associated with the Year 2000 problem:

- The potential expenses for litigation

- The risk of incurring possible damages through not fixing the Year 2000 problem

The four main kinds of Y2K-related litigation

In terms of the Year 2000 problem, at least four main types of litigation appear to be possible. Litigation could start as a result of:

- Injury or death sustained by any individual

- Action started by clients who lose money either directly or through damages sustained on their investments

- Dissatisfied shareholders of companies that suffer through the use of non-Y2K-compliant software

- Class action cases brought by customers who supposedly use compliant computer hardware or software, but which later turns out not to be

BEWARE In some **organisations,** especially those dealing with read-ahead date-related EDI-type processes, legal ramifications could become significant even before year 2000. Do take expert advice as soon as possible.

BEWARE If a user purchases some non-compliant software, but takes no steps to make it compliant, come year 2000, if our user decided to try and claim damages against the software maker, it's unlikely that an English court of law would be sympathetic.

REMEMBER Keep all records of management time and other costs spent in overcoming the Year 2000 problem.

Who may be affected?

If you or your organisation is blamed for some Year 2000-related error, whether directly or as an indirect consequence, the opposition's case for recovering costs and claiming financial compensation may prove a real threat. Two main areas might be of concern to readers of this book:

- *Suppliers*: computer systems suppliers have a responsibility to ensure that products certified as Y2K compliant really are fully Year 2000 compliant

- *Users:* those who use computer systems have a responsibility to ensure that they take steps to solve their Year 2000 problem in terms of how their systems interact with others. *Users have a duty to minimise any potential Year 2000-related affects that could damage or cause loss to other parties either directly or indirectly*

Who are those most likely to be affected?

As a general guide, let's first establish more precisely the potential main parties who could end up in court:

- Anyone who designs and produces computer software certified as Year 2000 compliant, but which turns out not to be

- Organisations offering Year 2000 certification

- Consultants who advise clients on Year 2000 issues and how to overcome any Y2K-related problems

- Year 2000 software vendors whose products don't live up to their promises

- Organisations who sell computer systems that are fully Y2K compliant but which 'don't meet the purpose for which they were intended'

- Directors and possibly senior management in any of the above organisations

Contracts and negligence

Users who consider they have a valid case, may try to recover some costs from a Year 2000-related supplier in two possible ways (at least), using:

The Latent Damage Act of 1986 stipulates that where claims for negligence involve a latent cause, a claim must be made within three years of discovery, or from the date when the defect should have been discovered.

- The Law of Contract (contract law)

- Tort of Negligence (negligence law)

Each of these methods is examined below.

The value of a contract

For claims under the Law of Contract, the implications could be particularly costly. The courts could allow for any or all of the following to apply:

- Recovery of loss through a *range* of different types of damages

- Allow a figure to cover *loss* of business profits

- Allow costs to cover the cost of *rectifying the problem*

So clearly, breaking a Year 2000-related contract in the eyes of the law could become an expensive mistake!

From a general legal standpoint, if you're prosecuting someone else, usually you have to provide evidence to prove the defendant has been negligent. So do keep all relevant documents and progress records relating to your Y2K status.

Implications for those who sell Y2K-related products

Remember, anyone who sells a product has a duty to ensure that *it is fit for the purpose for which it is intended.* Putting this in context of the Year 2000 problem, we could argue that an organisation not able to demonstrate *adequate* due care and attention is negligent. Therefore, what lawyers call the Tort of Negligence could apply here.

Even if let-off clauses are included in a contract between the parties, if lack of care and attention to the Year 2000 problem is established, the courts might consider such clauses to be irrelevant.

So in the Y2K legal context, what might the phrase 'Due care and attention' really mean? Certainly it does mean considering the broader issues involved and not acting in a reckless manner while providing professional advice or expert services.

Avoiding the outsourcing pitfall

If your organisation outsources IT-related work to another organisation, don't automatically assume your outsourcing contract will cover the complex and unforeseen Year 2000 ramifications.

REMEMBER

Outsourcing is where one organisation may employ a second organisation to carry out, on contract, part or all of its day-to-day computer-related operations. Outsourcing has become popular recently as a way of saving money and allegedly improving efficiency.

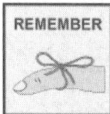

Some outsourcing organisations may accept liability. Most throwback problem back Check the your options. You could try to renegotiate your contract to share Year 2000-related costs.

limited however, use clauses to pass the to the host organisation. small print and evaluate

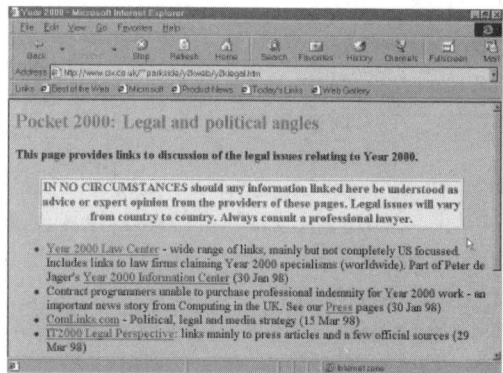

REMEMBER

Escrow is the legal term used to refer to a deed that only applies if a particular future event occurs. Check your dictionary to see a more general interpretation.

From the outsourcing point of view

Outsourcing companies may inherit non-compliant systems and their contracts may not include the all-important exclusion clauses. In this event, they could benefit by discussing any Year 2000-related problem with host clients and suppliers to avoid any possible costly litigation to all concerned later.

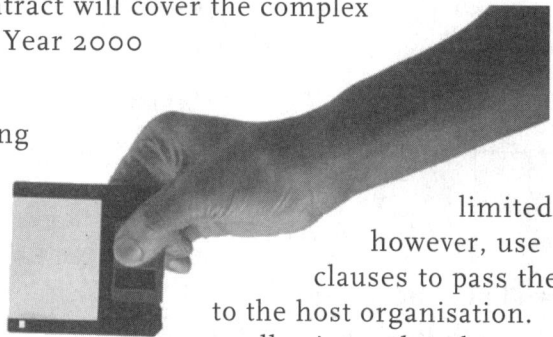

What if the worst happens ...?

Some Reasons for Y2K failure

We're not deliberately trying to appear downbeat, but sometimes Y2K repairs don't always go to plan. Here are some reasons why:

- Starting too late

- A lack of real commitment

- The shortage of trained programmers means that often there's not enough of the right people available

- Not allocating enough people and resources

- Not dealing with the problem properly: cutting corners to achieve a quick fix

- Not testing the repairs adequately enough: this is one of the most crucial areas for most organisations

- Not ensuring an adequate defence to prevent 'bad' data and non-compliant software from entering the new repaired Year 2000-compliant system

BEWARE Although perhaps unlikely, claims of Fraud may be made against non-Y2K-complying parties. However, these types of claim may be difficult to substantiate.

Devising a defence strategy should the worst happen

If as a result of some Year 2000-related problem, we're called to account, how do we best respond? First, put that very same question to your expert legal counsel. Arguably, perhaps the most important defence strategy is to be able to demonstrate a genuine caring desire to fix the problem and endorsing this by providing a structured plan with supporting documentary evidence of results obtained, to rid your organisation of the Year 2000 problem.

REMEMBER Create a log file containing details of what your organisation has done to overcome the Year 2000 problem. Ideally, this should include measures that clearly demonstrate a genuine desire to prevent Y2K-related damage occurring to others.

A growing trend to favour users

In recent years, where legal disputes have arisen between computer users and the opposing parties, there has been a tendency for the law courts to favour computer users, when attributing blame and apportioning costs. This trend can have serious implications for companies and organisations especially in terms of the Year 2000 problem. However, being forewarned is fore-armed.

Larger Organisations: Fight-back Planning

Larger organisations need a master plan to beat the bug. Many of the structured guidelines provided in Chapter 19 are particularly relevant to larger concerns. But in this chapter, we examine more closely the important aspect of planning from the perspective of large companies, institutions and other similar organisations.

Covers

Creating a survival plan

BEWARE **Any organisation considering taking** over another would do well to discover the target's current Y2K status/plans. Y2K compliancy can be a costly business and so affects the value of any asset.

BEWARE **Here's a list of the most important** kinds of business systems possibly affected by the Y2K problem: accounts receivable/payable, inventory control, payroll, employee pensions, licence issues, credit cards or anything involving date computations.

REMEMBER **If your organisation exchanges data** electronically, plan your Y2K repair strategy in consultation with all affected parties.

For larger companies and organisations, one of the most important things to realise is that devising a fix strategy can take several years and probably more staff than you have available. So the need for continued planning right the way through to repair and certification is essential.

Devising a general repair strategy is discussed in Chapter 19, step 3. However, where mission-critical applications are affected, the options discussed should be presented to senior management for evaluation and comparison within the context of any wider issues that may be relevant.

If you exchange data electronically ...

Contact your suppliers and ask them for a written statement of their Year 2000 compliance requirements from your hardware and software systems.

Likewise, you should draft your own statement and distribute it to all relevant suppliers and clients. This action achieves two things. It:

*   Clearly demonstrates your commitment to addressing the Year 2000 problem

*   Indicates that you're tackling the problem within your own organisation. This is reassuring to both clients and suppliers and gives them confidence to continue doing business with your organisation

Government departments and institutions

Many Y2K experts believe that most larger manufacturing and financial organisations will fare better than many government-related organisations come 2000. Why: simply because many of the movers and shakers in private enterprise now realise that they have to deal with the problem soon if they're to stay in business.

Often, government-backed bodies and the large institutions are the ones most in need of urgent Year 2000 repair. Here's why:

...cont'd

- Government- and institutional- based software systems are more likely than private enterprise to have older, more error- prone systems, in terms of the Year 2000 problem

- The priorities and working cultures between large institutions and private enterprise are often very different. Arguably, there's more of a sense of urgency within profit-driven private enterprises

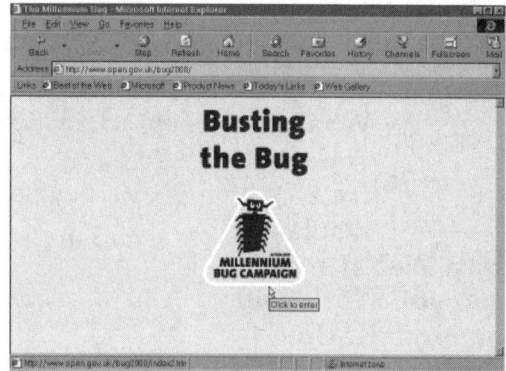

General guidelines

1 If you discover that your organisation has a Year 2000 problem, devise a plan to beat the bug and tell your employees so they know what to expect.

2 Also, tell your customers, so they too can establish a strategy to protect their systems. Note: they may also have similar problems – both could benefit from discussions.

3 Insist that your suppliers provide a written pledge stating that they can continue to provide their products and services reliably up to and beyond January 2000. They may also have Y2K problems; if so, you at least need to know about it.

4 With your legal experts, review your existing contracts with clients and suppliers. You should consider making changes where possible to your standard documentation and processes to minimise any legal liability.

Implementing your plan

For larger organisations, arguably the most important step is in acknowledging when there's a Year 2000 problem, and addressing the problem with in-depth and swift concrete action. Consider the following rough guidelines:

What is and what isn't displayed on a Web site can tell you a lot about an organisation. Smaller firms or suppliers that state their commitment and approach to beating the Y2K bug online also arguably demonstrate unusual openness, courage and originality.

1 Start by backing up your systems (see Chapter 3 for details). Also, make sure that your 'restore' routines work correctly.

2 Before performing any date roll-over tests, consider the cautions and guidelines provided in Chapter 16.

3 Make sure you have to hand all the original installation disks and CD-ROMs for any software installed on your systems. Although unlikely, it's possible that you may need to reinstall some software applications after testing.

4 If possible, print out your data files as a kind of insurance: a hard copy of your data is the ultimate backup. If the amount of data is large, and you don't want to print it all out, perform multiple backups instead and store at least one copy off-site.

Here's a list of typical business application software that may be affected: accounting, spreadsheets, databases, project management, financial tracking, and interest projection generators.

5 Perform the date roll-over tests for January 1st, 2000; February 28th, 2000 (leap year). Optionally, perform similar tests for the same dates in 2100 (not a leap year) to check for correct results.

6 Run some applications and perform some real-world tests. Choose applications that make particular use of dates or forward projections. Check the data results in depth.

7 If you have problems, determine where the problems lie: hardware, operating system or application software. Contact non-compliant application software vendors to find out how they can help you. Start planning in detail to beat the bug. Consider the issues outlined in this and other Year 2000-related sources, both in hard copy and on the Internet.

How Small Firms can Beat the Bug

Arguably, small businesses make up the group that are now at most risk from the Year 2000 problem. Some observers think the majority of small firms aren't taking the problem seriously enough with many heading for real trouble. Considering the enormous numbers of people employed in small concerns, the consequences could have far-reaching implications. In this chapter, we examine the Year 2000 problem from the small business perspective.

Covers

Chapter Thirteen

Why smaller firms are different

Many small firms use the Microsoft Windows 95/98, or NT operating systems. To find out the latest news about how these products comply, go to the Microsoft Year 2000 Resource Centre by pointing your Web browser at: http://www.microsoft.com/year2000/

What is and what isn't displayed on a Web site can tell you a lot about an organisation. If you deal with larger firms, log on to relevant Web sites to see if they state what their commitment to addressing their own Y2K problem is.

Come year 2000, some small firms are probably going to be in a lot of trouble with Y2K-related problems. The plain truth is that larger firms have deeper pockets, stronger resources and a greater 'bounce-back factor'. Most small firms, on the other hand don't have the access to a wide range of powerful resources. Also, many small firms have a carefully balanced cash flow: upsetting this can result in real, sometimes insurmountable problems.

But small firms have a lot going for them! They're often leaner, quicker and more flexible than large organisations. Employees of small firms often display strong cooperation, team spirit and a keen 'customer is king philosophy': all invaluable traits for beating the bug. Remember also, even if your firm doesn't use computers, you most likely will deal with someone who does: remember, the Year 2000 problem can affect many people in a variety of ways.

If you exchange data electronically ...

Having an electronic link to suppliers/clients brings an added urgency to overcoming any potential Y2K problems. Contact your suppliers and ask them for a written statement of their Year 2000 compliance requirements from your hardware and software. Likewise, you should draft your own statement and distribute it to all relevant suppliers and clients. This action achieves two things. It:

- Clearly demonstrates your commitment to addressing the Year 2000 bug

- Indicates that you're tackling the problem within your own organisation. This is reassuring to both clients and suppliers and gives them confidence to continue doing business with your organisation

Banking nerves spilling over onto small firms

The main banks are approaching small business customers and asking them to provide proof that they're Year 2000 compliant! Customers who fail or refuse to provide evidence risk having their overdrafts or other loans called in 1999! Start bug-busting today if you haven't already.

Success in five broad stages!

Microsoft say Windows 98 is fully Year 2000 compliant. Both Windows 95 and NT version 4.0 can recognise year 2000 but have 'some minor' problems.

If your organisation exchanges data electronically with outside parties, plan your Year 2000 repair strategy in consultation with those affected.

If you're in the UK, contact the Year 2000 Support Centre for advice. Their number is: 0800 146020. A fax-on-demand index digest is available on: 0870 908 2000 (touch-tone phones only).

It's important for managers in small firms to appreciate that the Y2K bug is not just a computer mainframe problem. We know it can affect any computer system and many electronic devices currently used in all sorts of industries (eg, electricity supplies, telephone systems, banks, stock markets, train systems, government agencies, planes and even some cars).

Learn some key knowledge. But whatever you do, if you haven't started already, make a start today. You may not even have a Year 2000 problem! Or your business may have a 'hidden' Year 2000 bug. You won't know until you look. Consider the following guidelines:

1. Learn about and discuss the Year 2000 problem, from your perspective, with colleagues, suppliers, clients, business clubs and associations; talk to your hardware supplier/maintainer; talk to your application software suppliers; get written guarantees for compliant components.

2. If you work under contract for a larger organisation, expect to receive a communication from them insisting that you make a legal statement of intention to comply. Prepare!

3. Consider at least discussing your outline problem with a reputable Year 2000 consultant, if you can. Sometimes, several tiny enterprises could benefit by combining their financial muscle to get the best deal.

4. If you identify that you have a Year 2000 problem, create a plan to beat it as soon as possible. Set a date for creating your plan and keep to it. Establish the date when you'll start running into problems if your Y2K problem is not put right.

5. Start implementing your plan as soon as possible; create a checklist and monitor progress every week; aim to have the problem cured at least 6 months before you expect the Time To Failure to occur (this is your fall-back safety margin).

...cont'd

HANDY TIP

If you have a Web site, stating your commitment and determination to beat the Y2K bug arguably demonstrates openness, courage and originality, *and provides an excellent advertisement to larger clients.*

Testing for the bug: precautions and procedures

The following guidelines outline a technical approach for dealing with the Year 2000 bug from the perspective of smaller organisations:

1   Start by backing up your systems (see chapter 3 for details). Also, make sure that your restore routines work correctly.

2   Before performing any date roll-over tests, read the cautions and guidelines provided in Chapter 16.

3   Make sure you have to hand all the original installation disks and CD-ROMs for any software installed on your systems. Although unlikely, it's possible that you may need to reinstall some software applications.

4   If possible, print out your data files as a kind of insurance: a hard copy of your data is the ultimate backup. If the amount of data is large, and you don't want to print it all out, perform multiple backups instead and store at least one copy off-site.

BEWARE

Don't perform any Year 2000 date roll-over tests if you have software licenses that might expire when you artificially move the current date forwards.

5   Perform the date roll-over tests for January 1st, 2000 and February 28th, 2000 (leap year). Optionally, perform similar tests for the same dates in 2100 (not a leap year) to check for correct results.

6   Run some applications and perform some real-world tests. Choose applications that make particular use of data or forward projections. Check the data results over several days if possible: the longer the test period, the better.

7   If you have problems, try to determine where the problems lie: hardware, operating system or application software, or all three. Contact non-compliant application software vendors to find out how they can help you.

Individual Computer Users

Everybody talks about the impact of the Year 2000 problem on companies and organisations: but what about individual computer users? If you use a computer at home or in an office to earn your living or simply to relax, then this chapter is for you.

Covers

Chapter Fourteen

An individual approach

REMEMBER

If your organisation exchanges data electronically with outside parties, plan your Year 2000 repair strategy in consultation with all those affected.

BEWARE

The high street banks are particularly concerned about the Y2K issue. They're already approaching their small business customers and asking them to provide proof that they're addressing the Y2K issue adequately. Customers who fail or refuse to provide evidence, risk having their overdrafts or other loans called in during 1999.

Most individuals who operate a small business or home office use a computer at least some of the time – even if only to print letters. But if you pass data on to work colleagues using floppy diskette, zip disk, CD-ROM, tape or in any other transferable form, you need to establish whether the date accuracy of this information impacts on the people you send it to – and if so, to what extent.

The simple answer is to make sure your computer is Year 2000 compliant. Remember, you may need to perform any or all of the following:

- Upgrade, change or replace computer hardware
- Purchase a Year 2000-compliant upgrade for your computer's operating system
- Purchase or obtain upgrades/fixes for application software
- Address the question of how to deal with archived data in the 'old' format, if this is important to your work

Taking the hard work out of testing and fixing

Specific Year 2000 software test products have already been developed to carry out things like testing for the date roll-over problem that may possibly be present on a PC. Some include routines to fix Y2K-related problems as well as providing some additional utilities. They range from basic PC testers to the more sophisticated network testing packages. Examples include: The Millennium Bug Toolkit from Computer Experts (01273 696975 or http:// www.computerexperts.co.uk) and Correx 2000 1.1 from Secure PC (0171 610 3646).

Computers for home and office use

If you use your computer for storing both work and personal data, remember you'll need to check the application and data files for both areas, in addition to application software, operating system and hardware.

Essential guidelines

Don't perform any Year 2000 date roll-over tests if you have software licenses that might expire when you artificially move the current date forwards. See Chapter 16 for more information.

Problems of working with a non-compliant computer

Anyone who uses a computer in their work to carry out basic word processing, graphics creation and DTP-type tasks may consider that inaccurate dates should not present much of a problem. But what about things like email?

These messages are date- and time-stamped. Inaccurate time- and date-stamps could have serious implications for those who accept orders for goods and services through email, especially if a dispute over work occurs at a later stage. Certain evidence might be considered legally invalid through inaccurate dating.

If you exchange data electronically

Many people send data directly to another organisation using phone lines or faster, higher quality ISDN-type connections.

Contact your suppliers and ask them for a written statement of their Year 2000 compliance requirements from your hardware and software.

Likewise, you should draft your own statement and distribute it to all relevant suppliers and clients. This action achieves two things. It:

- Clearly demonstrates your commitment to addressing the Year 2000 bug

- Indicates that you're tackling the problem. This is reassuring to both clients and suppliers and gives them confidence to continue doing business with you. Some larger clients may insist you address any Y2K-problems as a condition of continuing to do business with them

Make sure the Year 2000 repairs you perform ensure you can still match the data formats required by your suppliers and clients' computer systems.

Detecting and dealing with the Year 2000 bug

Individual computer users are often on their own when it comes to testing for and dealing with the Year 2000 problem. Consider the following guidelines:

1   First, back up your computer (see chapter 3 for details). Also, make sure that your 'restore' routines work correctly.

2   Before performing the date roll-over tests, read the cautions and guidelines provided in Chapter 16.

3   Make sure you have to hand all the original installation disks and CD-ROMs for any software installed on your systems. Although unlikely, it's possible that you may need to reinstall some software applications.

HANDY TIP

If your hardware is not up to dealing with the Year 2000 problem, consider the guidelines provided in Chapter 20: *Purchasing Hardware and Software.*

4   If possible, print out your important data files. This activity is a kind of insurance: a hard copy of your data is the ultimate backup. If the amount of data is large, then you probably won't want to print out everything. In this event, perform multiple backups instead. Keep one copy elsewhere.

5   Perform the date roll-over tests in Chapter 16 for January 1st, 2000 and February 28th, 2000 (leap year). Optionally, perform similar tests for the same dates in 2100 (not a leap year) to check for correct results.

6   Run some applications and perform some real-world tests. Choose applications that make particular use of data or forward projections. Check the accuracy of the results.

7   If you have problems, try to determine where the problem lies: hardware, operating system or application software, or all three. Contact non-compliant application software vendors to find out how they can help you.

Benefits of Achieving Y2K Compliance

The Year 2000 problem is without doubt complex and successfully overcoming it requires a closely managed approach with painstaking attention to detail. But for those who meet the compliance conditions, clear benefits emerge. This chapter identifies some of the ways in which you can gain by successfully overcoming one of the most formidable business problems of the 20th century.

Covers

Chapter Fifteen

Nine *benefits* of beating the bug

Considering all the possible problems associated with the Year 2000 bug, is it really all worth it? Benefits of Year 2000 compliance can be many and varied – some are obvious, others are perhaps unexpected.

Also, some will gain more than others, but the following list provides a broad view of the most obvious advantages of compliance:

REMEMBER

A more precise and concise definition of Y2K compliance is simply any system that can handle all dates without any ambiguity in both the 20th and 21st centuries.

- The big one: a greater likelihood of *remaining in business* after January 1st, 2000

- *Reduced litigation costs*. The expected cost of not achieving Year 2000 compliance in terms of possible litigation, reputation and other types of 'damage' could amount to more than ten or twenty times the cost of successful Year 2000 repair!

- *Possible sales boost for almost zero direct effort*. A Year 2000-compliant organisation will be better positioned to benefit the clients of those competitors who don't address their own Y2K problems adequately

- An *increased awareness of your own software*, its advantages, drawbacks and its limitations

- Achieving Y2K compliance could generally help create a *more stable and streamlined software base*

- Should result in *better documented core software code* that is *easier to update and maintain*

- *Reduced software maintenance costs*. Y2K bug correction requires key software maintenance to be carried out sooner rather than later. The chances are, this update/maintenance work would probably have to be done at some stage anyway. Costs usually keep rising, so doing it now could save a considerable sum later

- *New software tools*. The extra investment in software tools purchased need not be wasted as these tools could be used for other purposes at a later stage

- One of the most unlikely benefits of beating the Year 2000 bug is *litter removal*. Any older and no longer used code present in your systems can be removed, creating more effective and possibly faster software

Turn the Year 2000 problem on its head!

Although the Year 2000 bug can create enormous problems for some organisations:

It can also serve as a link which can bind you closer to your customers.

REMEMBER

In many older computer systems, often there are thousands of lines of code that have never been used in years. Establish the last time each code module was used, and on that basis you can decide whether to keep or delete the unnecessary code.

For business-oriented readers, the above sentence can become a powerful marketing concept as we'll see overleaf.

One thing is for certain, the Year 2000 problem will remain in the minds of those who are closest to it for many years to come. So if your organisation has made its mark, a positive impression in the minds of your existing clients and perhaps more importantly, in the minds of potential prospects, they won't easily forget your approach and eventual success in beating the Year 2000 problem.

Often, your customers are like you, feeling the pain of dealing with the bug and all parties involved can identify with the experiences of others in similar circumstances.

And remember, the plain truth is that by the end of year 2000, if as an organisation or business individual you've overcome any Year 2000 problems, the insidious nature of the problem will probably mean you'll have fewer competitors with which to compete against for at least three or four years.

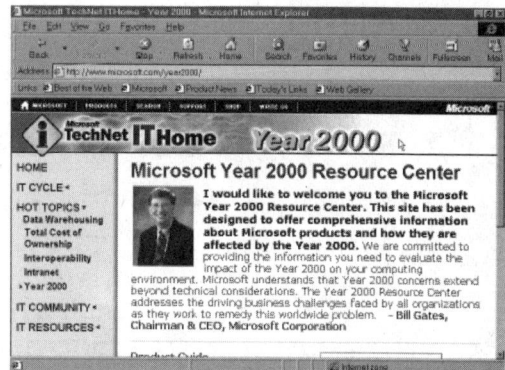

Marketing your Year 2000 success

Any organisation that solves its own Year 2000 problem with plenty of time to spare is without doubt special. And any organisation or individual in business who also beats the bug at any time deserves to build on that success. And why not? That's what marketing is all about!

In fact, effectively marketing your Year 2000 success can bring enormous benefits. Let's examine this subject more closely.

It's not a walk in the park!

By the time we're about half way through 1999, many key people in organisations large and small across the globe will know that overcoming the Year 2000 problem is 'no walk in the park'.

If we view the Year 2000 problem at face value, collectively we see millions, probably billions being spent on something that only allows us, at best, to stay in business – a zero return on a high cost investment.

But it need not be like that.

The fact that enormous sums are being spent on an apparent zero return means it's not a bad idea to look at ways in which to build on that success in a positive way.

Let's look at some ways in which an organisation that successfully overcomes the Year 2000 bug before it becomes a 'problem' can turn the entire mess into a highly successful marketing campaign:

- Offer practical to help customers who are struggling with the Year 2000 problem. By helping a customer in some concrete way, you're positioning yourself uniquely: the chances are your efforts, whatever the outcome, will be remembered for some time to come

- Share information and advice, and keep in touch. Perhaps send out a regular newsletter that is finely tuned for each client's needs. Regularly contact key representatives, ask about progress and look for ways in which you can make tangible contributions

HANDY TIP

Another way in which you can help your customers is to put essential key information on your Web site. Provide them with restricted keyword access, so that only those people you want to view this part of your Web site get to see the goodies.

Testing PC Hardware for the Y2K Bug

This chapter contains some of the most practical information in the book. Here you can learn how to check your PC hardware for the presence of the Year 2000 problem by performing a simple test sequence. But BEFORE you start, please do read the preliminary pages.

Covers

Chapter Sixteen

CAUTION: READ ME FIRST

If you want to perform the Year 2000 roll-over test on your main 'production' PC, allow yourself plenty of time. Don't rush and try to make sure you're not interrupted while you perform the test.

Before performing the Year 2000 test on page 119, make sure you've backed up everything on your PC. Chapter 3, *Backing up Your Systems*, examines this important activity in more depth.

When testing software applications, run tests ideally over a period of several weeks if possible, to ensure correct dates do appear.

The simplest and most obvious way to test if a PC can handle year 2000 dates and beyond properly is to temporarily move the date on your PC forward. However, you need to be careful. If specific parts of your computer system are not Year 2000 compliant, here's what could happen:

- Your data could become damaged or even deleted

- Leased-, demonstration-, or evaluation-type software with time limits on usage could expire or be permanently disabled

- Some dated software security certificates could become invalid

- Email messages could be misfiled

- Your calendar-based software could ignore or even delete important appointment dates automatically and you may not know this has happened

So what should you do? First, you need to check if you have any time-limited software installed on your servers or PCs. If you have, DON'T CARRY OUT THE TESTS ON PAGE 119. Instead, contact your supplier or software vendor and ask their advice about performing the Year 2000 date roll-over test.

Use a test PC if possible

Microsoft go further: they advise that you only perform a Year 2000 roll-over test on a test PC, not on a production PC. This way, if problems do occur, your day-to-day PC activities should not be affected. You can then determine where the problem lies on the test PC. This is obviously good advice. If you have access to another, similar PC to the one you really want to test, then certainly follow this route if possible.

Often, however, this option is simply not available. In that event, it's always a good idea to check with your PC supplier/manufacturer first. And please do consider the guidelines provided in this chapter.

Different date formats

Although this chapter refers mainly to the PC, here's some guidelines to consider for testing any computer system for the Year 2000 bug. (1) Even if your computer appears to be OK, check your data to ensure it hasn't become corrupted. (2) Run the roll-over test for the equivalent dates in 2001, just to be sure.

The Year 2000 problem is not affected by changing the date *format* used in your computer. The standard UK date format is DD/MM/YYYY, and those in the US often prefer MM/DD/YYYY. In Windows, you can use the format suggested for your country.

Several different standards exist across the globe for displaying dates and times. The better operating systems allow you to use the time and date format you prefer. Windows 95/98, for example, allows you to set your desired date format using the Regional Settings and Date/Time icons in the Control Panel.

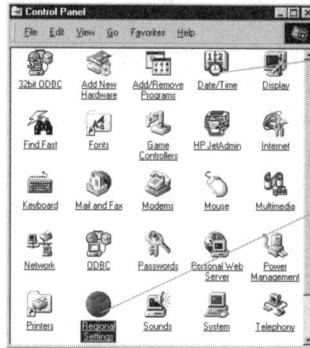

Click here to set the Date/Time properties

Click here to set the Regional Settings properties

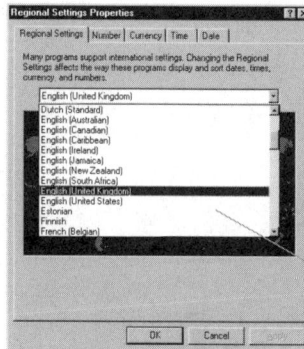

The Windows Date/Time Properties dialog box

The Regional Settings Properties dialog box showing some of the date options available

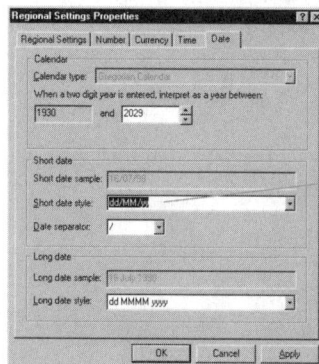

Setting the UK date format

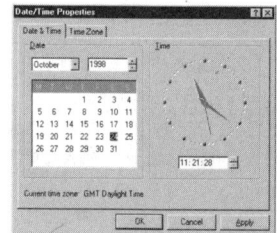

The need for PC Start-up disks

Frustrating, isn't it: when you need your Windows 98 Start-up disk, you can't find it. You think you remember placing it with your operating system diskettes or CD-ROMs. But when you look, it's not there. You certainly won't be alone.

However, when subjecting a PC to the Year 2000 assault course, sometimes unexpected results can occur. And it may turn out that your Windows 98 Start-up disk, or any other emergency Start-up diskettes you need, are all that is necessary to help get you up and running once again.

You probably won't need them, but the point of this page is to prompt you to have your Start-up diskettes and CD-ROMs close by in case you do. Here's how to make a Windows 95/98 Start-up disk if you've not already done so:

1 Click the Start button followed by Settings, then Control Panel.

2 Select the Add/Remove Programs icon.

3 Click the Startup Disk tab.

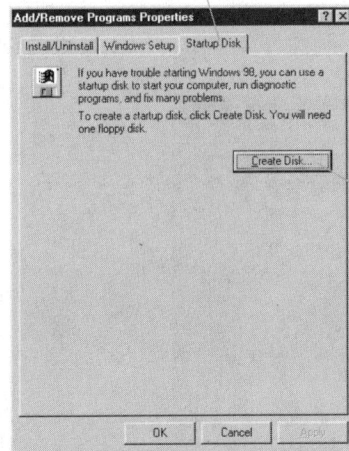

4 Insert a blank floppy diskette (or one containing files you don't want to keep) into your disk drive.

5 Click the Create Disk button.

6 Follow onscreen instructions.

7 Remove and label the Start-up disk; store in a secure location.

Performing the test

REMEMBER **If you use Microsoft Windows, in the test outlined on this page you can set the date in the Control Panel rather than at the DOS prompt if you prefer. The DOS prompt method was chosen as a 'standard' approach for readers who may be using pure MS-DOS, Windows 3.XX, Windows 95/98, or any other compatible front end.**

To check your PC hardware BIOS and operating system for the presence of the Y2K problem, here's what you do:

1 If the PC is connected to a network, you need to isolate it from the network. However, do discuss this with your network administrator *before* unplugging or disconnecting any PC.

2 Next, you need to close down any open programs and display the DOS prompt. If Windows has already started, choose the command to shut down and 'Restart in MS-DOS Mode'.

3 In a few seconds, you should see the DOS prompt as something like this: C:\ (assuming that C: is the hard drive that loads your operating system when you first switch on – this is your 'boot' drive). Otherwise, you'll see the particular letter of the drive you're booting up from.

REMEMBER **When performing this kind of test, it's arguably better to enter the date directly at the DOS prompt. This date is usually read from your BIOS chip. Your application software uses this reference for all relevant date- and time-related calculations.**

```
Microsoft(R) Windows 95
    (C)Copyright Microsoft Corp 1981-1995.

C:\WINDOWS>date
Current date is Thu 06/08/1998
Enter new date (dd-mm-yy): 31-12-1999

C:\WINDOWS>date
Current date is Fri 31/12/1999
Enter new date (dd-mm-yy):

C:\WINDOWS>time
Current time is  13:13:18.65
Enter new time: 23:58

C:\WINDOWS>time
Current time is  23:58:01.68
Enter new time: _
```

4 At the keyboard, type DATE and press the ENTER key. Windows prompts you to enter a new date. The date you want is December 31st, 1999. If you're using the UK date format, type: 31-12-99. If you're using the US date format, type: 12-31-99. Then press the ENTER key again.

5 (Optional) To confirm that you've entered the new date correctly, type DATE again. Windows displays the date you entered. Press the ENTER key to reaccept your entry.

...cont'd

REMEMBER

The term workstation originally applied to powerful UNIX terminals (usually containing no hard drive) connected to a computer network (LAN). However, nowadays many people refer to a workstation as simply any PC connected to a LAN.

REMEMBER

If your operating system is not MS- DOS and you want to determine how it will deal with dates beyond December 31st, 1999, contact your software maker or supplier and ask them. Have the version number of your operating system ready. If you're doubtful, ask them to provide a written statement of the date limit.

6 Next, type the word TIME then press the ENTER key. If you're using the 24-hour time format, enter 23:58. If you're using the 12-hour format, type 11:58.

```
Microsoft(R) Windows 95
   (C)Copyright Microsoft Corp 1981-1995.

C:\WINDOWS>date
Current date is Thu 06/08/1998
Enter new date (dd-mm-yy): 31-12-1999

C:\WINDOWS>date
Current date is Fri 31/12/1999
Enter new date (dd-mm-yy):

C:\WINDOWS>time
Current time is  13:13:18.65
Enter new time: 23:58

C:\WINDOWS>time
Current time is  23:58:01.68
Enter new time: _
```

7 (Optional) To confirm that you've entered the time value correctly, type TIME then press the ENTER key again.

8 Now switch the PC off and wait at least 3 or 4 minutes. Then switch it back on and display the DOS prompt as described in steps 2 and 3 on the previous page.

9 Type the DATE command again to view the date. If your PC displays Saturday, January 1st, 2000, go to step 10. If any other date or condition is displayed, go to step 11.

10 Perform steps 4–7 again, but this time leave your PC switched on. Wait 3 or 4 minutes, then type DATE and press the ENTER key. If the date correctly displays Saturday, January 1st, 2000, congratulations! – your PC has passed the test. Go to step 12. Otherwise go to step 11.

11 A non-compliant PC will probably show 1/4/1980 – January 4, 1980 (MS-DOS's birthday) or some other incorrect date. This PC would appear *not* to be compliant. Record the model, serial number and type of failure. Speak to your supplier to examine your options. Now do step 12.

12 Now return your PC back to its original condition: perform steps 4–7 above but re-enter the correct current date and time, then restore any auto-startup programs and, optionally, re-connect to your network.

Choosing Y2K Consultants and Repairers

There's now a lot of help available for those who think they may have a Year 2000 problem. But who do you ask and how do you go about finding people you can rely on. This chapter examines what you need to be aware of when contracting a Y2K consultant. We also take a look at how repair vendors can help your organisation.

Covers

Why bother hiring a consultant?

Here's a well-worn cliche: 'Good consultants are worth their weight in gold'. In terms of the Year 2000 problem, this is true for sure. Consultants cost money, but a good consultant can save you much more than you pay them. Consider the following guidelines:

What a good consultant can provide

REMEMBER

A Y2K consultant provides advice on Year 2000 issues affecting your organisation. Contrast this definition with 'Y2K tool vendor' in the margin of page 126.

- An objective view of your project. Often, your own people can be too close to the real issues to think them through properly

- Right from the outset, a view of the big picture can be given without emotion or bias

- A more watertight approach: if several people are working on the project, each in their own field, it's difficult to watch everything properly

- A consultant can look at the general direction of the project as well as attending to specific details

HANDY TIP

Here's some added value: you can apply and modify the techniques described in this chapter relating to choosing a consultant, for any project you're involved in, not just Year 2000 issues.

- A realisation of things you may never have thought of before they can cause additional problems

- An independent consultant has no secret agenda

- Greater experience: the chances are, your consultant has already been involved in Y2K projects and so already has real experience of beating the bug

- If bad news is going to result in sackings, it's better coming from a consultant rather than from an employee: the employee has more to lose

But here are some drawbacks ...

- A good consultant is going to ask a lot of questions. Some friction may result, but be patient: if they do their job correctly, it'll all be worth it!

- To begin with, they'll need time to learn about your systems and your business. They'll need to talk with the relevant people during this phase

Characteristic indicators

What can a good consultant really offer you? What can you look for to try and secure the best return on your investment? These and other questions must enter the minds of those people charged with this responsibility. Here are some more key guidelines:

- How do you know they really are who they say they are: first check that the person you're thinking of hiring really is a Year 2000 consultant. A mistake here could cost you dearly

- Considered use of appropriate software tools can help speed up any Year 2000 repair program. A good consultant has an in-depth knowledge of what is available and what is appropriate to your situation

HANDY TIP **Any consultant recommended by someone you know and trust, and who ideally has already employed them, is usually the best recommendation you can hope for. However, don't weaken: still check the validity of your preferred consultant's credentials.**

Hiring independent consultants

Year 2000 consultants may be totally independent or allied to another organisation. However, remember that there are many reputable tied consultants, but tied status must impact on their decision-making and advice. This may be perfectly fine for your project: you should just be aware of the differences. Nevertheless, here's two important points to consider when hiring an independent consultant:

- This person is arguably more likely to offer a more objective, customer-oriented service

- Try to assess whether your proposed consultant displays any get-rich-quick giveaway signs. This one's difficult, but considering things like, attitude, demeanour, even body language, and so on, can help

Finding a reputable consultant

Considering how vulnerable your data and software code is during the Year 2000 repair phase, the big question is: how do you find a reputable, trustworthy consultant? And how do you know that the consultant you're hiring really can do the job.

The short answer is, of course, you don't – you can never be 100% sure. Nevertheless, there are certain things you can do to at least weed out those consultants who may not really help your cause. The Year 2000 problem is a one-shot arena: you have one chance to get it right! So if you're planning to hire a consultant, you need to be as sure as you can that the person you're hiring is right for you. Consider asking your short list of consultants the following key questions:

REMEMBER

If your computer systems aren't too complex, you may not need a full-blown (probably expensive) Y2K consultant. You may find a good, reliable, non-specialised local consultant who can help you in identifying the problem areas and suggest some software tools which may be used to cure much of the problem for you.

1 *'Can you guarantee that with your help we'll become 100% Year 2000 compliant?'* If they say yes, you know they're either lying or they don't have the experience you're looking for. No one can guarantee 100% that you'll have no Y2K-related problems – the bug is just too complex.

HANDY TIP

By asking open-ended questions, you're testing a consultant's knowledge further and reducing the chance that they may simply 'guess' correctly.

2 *'What other Year 2000 projects have you worked on?'* This may sound obvious but the Year 2000 problem has become a gold mine of opportunity for just about anyone who knows a little more than the average person in the street. Some can be convincing, but you need proof: ideally, documentary evidence and verifiable testimonials relating to previous Y2K projects are ideal.

3 *'Were you involved in creating the Year 2000 problem?'* If a consultant denies having any involvement in causing the problem, the chances are they don't have enough experience to fix it properly. Often, the best people to cure a problem are those that were involved in creating it.

Choosing repair vendors

Repair vendors provide services in some or all areas concerning the Year 2000 problem. Some of the most common services available include:

- Systems inventory and audit

- Code analysis

- Y2K impact analysis

- Conversion assessment, planning and estimating

- Code repair

- Year 2000 repair testing

- General consultation and advice

HANDY TIP
One way to save time and money, and allow your own staff to concentrate on new plans, is to outsource your entire Year 2000 repair project. Bottom Line: you need to have confidence in the organisation you choose.

HANDY TIP
Compile a list of key questions to put to prospective Year 2000 repair organisations. Check out references they provide. Ensure they can fit in with your way of working.

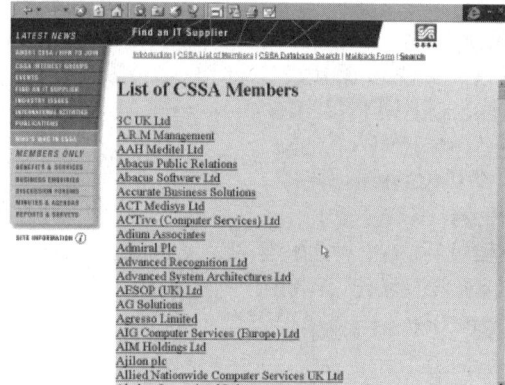

Some specialise in specific languages, platforms, operating systems, or other areas. Some use preferred Year 2000 repair tools and include the cost of these in the deal, while others charge extra.

Some base their prices on the total number of Lines Of Code (LOC) involved, while others use a combination of variables to work out a price.

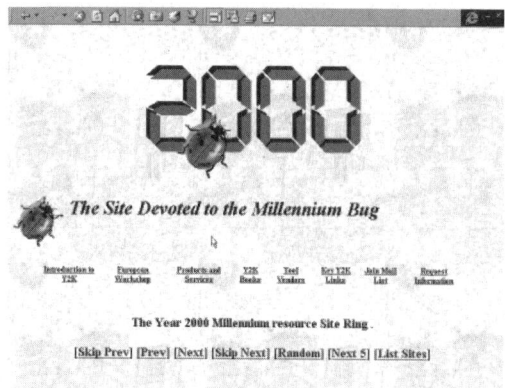

If your organisation doesn't have enough time, resources or people available to fix the Y2K bug internally, a reputable repair vendor may provide the extra staff and resources required.

REMEMBER

A Y2K tool vendor can provide advice on the wide range of software tools available to help combat the Year 2000 problem. Contrast this definition with 'Y2K consultant' in the margin of page 122.

HANDY TIP

Many Y2K repair vendors advertise their services on their Web sites. The tone of a Web site can often be a useful indicator about the quality and approach of an organisation. View a prospect's Web site before contacting them to gain a greater insight into their approach.

However, the use of an outside organisation coupled with the importance of Year 2000 issues, highlights certain aspects. For example:

- Do a prospective repair vendor's people truly understand how the seriousness of the Year 2000 problem impacts on your organisation? Many repair vendors carry out other types of support work also. Therefore, there's a danger that they may simply not be up to the job

- What assurances can they give you if their own key specialists become sick?

Security: working with your repair vendor

Ideally, choose a repair vendor from personal recommendation or one with a demonstrable reputable track record.

Some repair vendors may offer to take your code away and work on it at their own premises. Although this approach can save money, you should be aware of the increased security risk to your code and data.

However, even if a repair vendor is working on-site at your premises, there's still a risk that – using their own hardware – data and code copies could still be taken. Most repair vendors are probably honourable, but you still need to be aware of the negative possibilities and therefore remain cautious and alert.

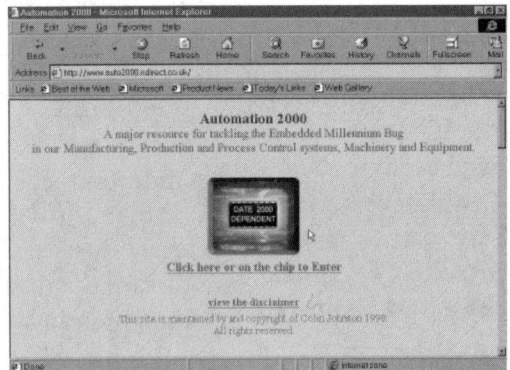

Year 2000 People Aspects

We can focus on the Year 2000 problem in terms of hardware and software remedies and costs. But all too often it's easy to underestimate the real effects on the people closest to the problem. This chapter examines these issues: how we can reassess the people who work in our organisations, and how to retain their loyalty beyond 2000.

Covers

Chapter Eighteen

How the Y2K bug affects people

It's not the buildings, the products or the usually expensive IT infrastructure that makes an organisation successful: it's the people. Employees are the lifeblood of any successful business or organisation today.

Of course, all of these other components are essential, but people are special because of the level of creativity, resourcefulness and applied intelligence they can bring to bear on the Year 2000 problem. In fact, it's usually these same traits that contribute much to the business of creating successful organisations.

The Year 2000 problem affects different people in different ways. Consider:

REMEMBER

If your organisation has a Year 2000 problem, the employees should be told about this as soon as possible: only then can they help. Employee participation is crucial to overcoming the Year 2000 problem.

- The Year 2000 problem can understandably make people edgy: the prospect of the unknown can unsettle people. The problem is complex and this is often made worse by media hype

- Low morale may become a problem if employees feel their jobs are at risk (but remember, sometimes this same fear can help improve poor teamworking ability and increase motivation).

- Employees can benefit from being kept informed of Year 2000 repair progress on a regular basis. This approach helps ease their concerns and can help prevent false negative rumours spreading

- Some gain considerably: like repair vendors and Y2K consultants

...cont'd

...cont'd

- Those who work for organisations that pledge to repair their computer systems often have to endure even greater pressures and stresses

- Forward thinking managers could make allowances for occasional outbursts and suggest everybody concerned should meet regularly to discuss ways to ease the burden for all, while still getting the job done. People then have a chance to air grievances

- Those organisations that beat the bug can arguably come through potentially as leaner, fitter and more efficient: some older software systems may be retired; other software may be upgraded/updated, and this sort of activity often speeds things up. These kinds of results usually have a positive effect on employees

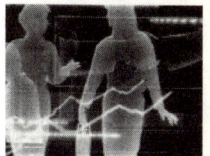

HANDY TIP

By being up front with employees right from the start about the seriousness and possible consequences of any Y2K-related issues and then keeping them informed of progress, a stronger team spirit can emerge.

Year 2000   50 Excuses

Fifty ways to resolve your date-handling problems?

Micro Focus' Challenge 2000 (with all of its components and consulting partners) provides the flexibility to solve your customers year 2000 problems. Below (courtesy of Peter de Jager, pdejager@year2000.com) are 50 reasons why you (or your boss) may be ignoring the year 2000 problem.

The 50 Reasons Why You Are Ignoring The Year 2000 Problem

1. It's someone else's problem.

2. Someone smarter than you will come up with an automated solution.

3. You're planning to retire next year.

4. You just don't have the time right now. Ask me again next year when things slow down.

5. You want to surprise your stockholders.

Assessing the real value of key staff

Some staff are going to be crucial in solving any Year 2000 problems. These people need to be identified right at the outset of a Year 2000 repair project.

Establishing a Year 2000 problem-solving team

Here the key job is to select the most appropriate people for each role. Sometimes, that is easy to say but difficult to implement.

Faced with the question of who do you choose, one useful approach is to turn the situation around: ask yourself who in your organisation would eventually be charged with sorting the problem out if it was left unrepaired. When you have some names, those are ideal people to include on your Year 2000 project team.

Here's a list of typical roles:

- Project manager/team leader(s)

- Outside consultant: to help provide a more objective, independent viewpoint and to help coordinate the project as a whole

- Applications programmer: to ensure all your commercial-off-the-shelf applications are updated

- Bespoke software programmer: to handle all code developed specially for your organisation

- Data person: someone who is responsible for converting your data

- Support systems person: to handle all the backup and support systems conversions

- Test engineer(s): to ensure that repairs, conversions and updates are valid

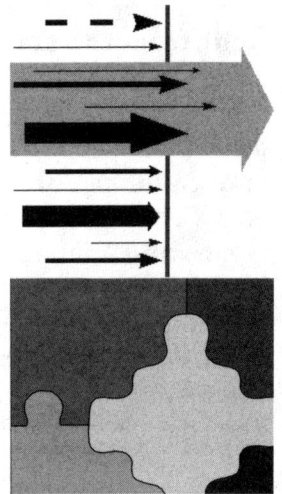

Keeping staff loyal beyond 2000

REMEMBER

The Y2K bug has created a seller's market: some employees with special skills are suddenly in high demand. However, this may only last 2–3 years.

HANDY TIP

When considering ways to keep key staff, try applying some psychology. It's true people are highly motivated by money, but sometimes other things are equally important. Try to learn about your employees as individuals to gauge their value mechanisms. For example: job status, company perks, flexible work choices, pension deals, and so on. Brainstorm for new ideas.

Approaching the end of this millennium while repairing non-compliant computer systems is a tense business. People's jobs are unavoidably affected – some more than others. However, it's even more essential to keep on board those key people who 'keep the wheels turning'. Key IT staff are also aware of this apparently sudden change of their employment status and may be tempted to look further afield.

One thing is almost certainly true: under current estimates, there are probably not going be enough suitable people to carry out all the repairs necessary. Those larger organisations that have ignored the Year 2000 problem may find they'll need to have a large reserve of extra money quickly, if they're to beat the bug at this late stage.

They'll probably need to poach key staff from competitors or other firms. Some organisations are probably heading for some nasty shocks as key staff may be approached by competitor organisations with offers of double or even triple their present salaries on a three-year contract basis.

So how do we ensure we keep key staff – particularly those in IT departments – loyal through the coming few years. Once the change-over date to the new millennium has been completed successfully, the pressure will of course ease and the employment marketplace will probably change yet again. But these coming two years require a steady course. Here are some ideas to help you retain your key staff:

- Accept that the true worth of key employees has increased dramatically, simply because of the millennium bug. It may be unfair to others who may have perhaps made a greater contribution, but this is the reality today and the bug can threaten an entire organisation's survival

- Treat all employees with respect and fairness

- Consider offering going-rate lucrative pay deals and other perks (shares for example) in return for a legally signed pledge to stay for, say, three years-plus

HANDY TIP **By offering some sort of share/ stock ownership deal to key IT employees to encourage them to stay, you're strengthening further their future prosperity with the survival of the company. This can provide a highly motivating 'stay' mechanism.**

BEWARE **The Year 2000 bug creates tension. But organisations that bully staff into solving the problem 'after hours' may not gain the best output or command staff loyalty. Organisations that treat their staff well may enter the new millennium as the biggest gainers.**

How there's new value for older workers

In addition to staff loyalty, a range of other issues could affect your key staff levels. To ensure successful conversion of older systems, like those using COBOL for example, you'll probably need to draw on the skills of older programmers. But several questions emerge:

- How many of these older programmers who really know about this type of software are still on the payroll?

- Of those, how many are available to work on the Year 2000 problem?

- And how many are nearing retirement age?

- Can some retired previous employees be tempted to come out of retirement to help solve the problems?

- What prospect is there of some retired previous employees working part-time from home?

Many companies and organisations will no doubt be asking similar questions of their current and retired employees, and so there may well be shortages of key personnel. Some organisations may find they can meet all their extra capacity needs simply by applying the ideas mentioned in the last two items in the list above.

How flexible things break less

The point is, a flexible operation has arguably more chance of success, even if it does mean grappling sooner with the new management methods that are emerging – like teleworking – rather than in five years time, when such work practices are expected to become much more commonplace than they are today.

How to Beat the Y2K Bug in Six Steps

For companies and organisations of all sizes, this chapter provides a universal plan that you can fine-tune to your own needs. Here, we show how you can overcome the Year 2000 problem in six clearly defined steps.

Covers

Chapter Nineteen

The six-step approach at a glance

To quickly get a clearer picture of what's covered in this chapter, let's take a brief look at the six steps outlined.

BEWARE

Businesses will endure some 'hot' Y2K-related dates. For example: those around the financial year end and any tax-related dates. In this way, some organisations may be affected by the Y2K problem as early as 1998/99.

Step 1: Becoming aware

This step is about determining if an organisation has a Year 2000 problem, and if so demonstrating to management how and when the Y2K problem will become active.

Step 2: Assessing what is required

Assessing what you need to do to overcome the Year 2000 problem is often the hardest part. This step essentially deals with how to find out precisely what may be affected in your organisation, the importance of planning and time allocation in determining how much time you've got to repair or replace your computer systems.

HANDY TIP

Try to agree to have dates sent across program interfaces in four-digit format.

Step 3: Creating a repair strategy

This step lists the most common approaches for dealing with the Year 2000 problem and highlights the one crucial area to watch: program interfaces. Step 3 also helps you to decide what to repair first by establishing priorities.

Step 4: Demonstrating how it works

Once you've decide how you're going to repair each area of your organisation's systems, next you need to know that your methods will work. The step is really all about the importance of thorough testing and how the best approach involves performing a pilot test to resolve most of the unforeseen problems before full implementation.

HANDY TIP

When testing repaired software, run tests ideally over a period of several weeks.

Step 5: Implementing your strategy

By this stage, you're ready to make it happen. This stage stresses the importance of timing and the need for further operational testing.

Step 6: Staying alert

Step 6 is all about protecting your repairs once they're active. It's about considering and establishing procedures and protocols to prevent any 'bad' old-style data entering your computer systems.

HANDY TIP

Exercise tight centralised management control to overcome the Y2K problem more effectively.

...cont'd

The six-step approach: a graphical interpretation

HANDY TIP

Adopt a repetitive approach. The testing phase involves repeating routines in several different ways.

BEWARE

Don't underrate testing. By identifying and fixing the problems before your customer finds them, you're probably going to save money.

REMEMBER

Regression-test your repaired systems using a wide range of test data. Especially test the limits of a system.

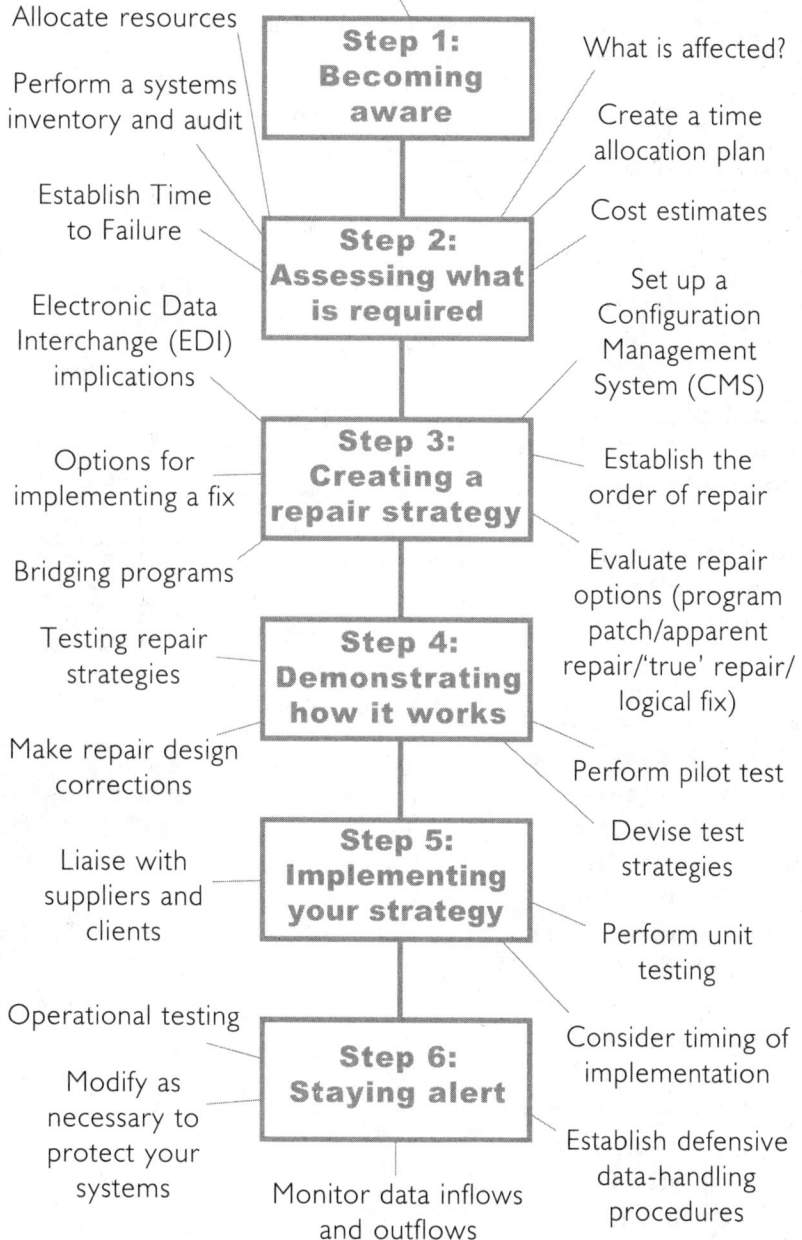

Is there a problem – how big is it?

Allocate resources

Perform a systems inventory and audit

Step 1: Becoming aware

What is affected?

Create a time allocation plan

Establish Time to Failure

Step 2: Assessing what is required

Cost estimates

Set up a Configuration Management System (CMS)

Electronic Data Interchange (EDI) implications

Options for implementing a fix

Step 3: Creating a repair strategy

Establish the order of repair

Bridging programs

Testing repair strategies

Step 4: Demonstrating how it works

Evaluate repair options (program patch/apparent repair/'true' repair/ logical fix)

Make repair design corrections

Perform pilot test

Liaise with suppliers and clients

Step 5: Implementing your strategy

Devise test strategies

Perform unit testing

Operational testing

Modify as necessary to protect your systems

Step 6: Staying alert

Consider timing of implementation

Establish defensive data-handling procedures

Monitor data inflows and outflows

Step 1: Becoming aware

HANDY TIP Managers usually listen if you can demonstrate in *specific, relevant* terms how the Y2K problem will impact their organisation.

This first step is often the most difficult for technical people as it's not really a technical step. Often, technical people like to jump straight into the actual conversion process. Resist this approach and follow a structured program starting with a comprehensive initial analysis.

Convincing management there's a problem

Becoming aware of the problem is essentially a people-oriented step. This step is mainly management territory. It's here that management need to understand the real, dire implications of doing nothing.

HANDY TIP Consider setting up a Year 2000 problem-solving team, with the right people to see it through and ensure the repair plan is implemented properly and on time.

But to take effective decisions, managers need hard facts that are relevant to their organisation, not the general and often overblown excerpts from the media. Managers need to know four essential things about any potential Year 2000 problem:

- Whether their organisation *has* a Y2K problem

- If so, how big is it?

HANDY TIP Computer systems are one of the most valuable assets of any organisation, yet few know much about their own systems. If you can take the time to learn about yours, you'll position your organisation better to deal with the Y2K problem.

- An assessment of the risks to the organisation if the problem is not fixed

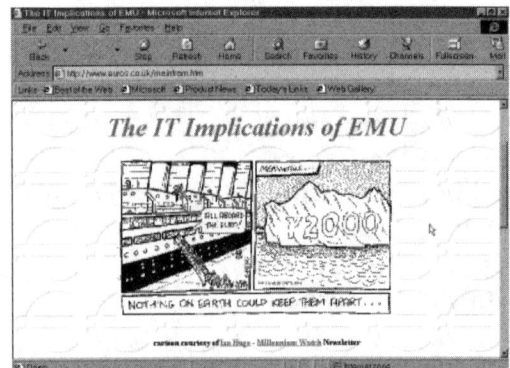

...cont'd

HANDY TIP
Although methods and protocols can be set up to deal with the Year 2000 problem, don't forget teamwork and a genuine desire to beat the bug are two of the most effective tools any organisation can bring to bear on the problem.

REMEMBER
Year 2000 project managers are going to be busy people. Here's a list of some key strategies they'll need to be concerned with: starting off, financing the repair, keeping staff and clients happy, minimising disruption during repair, resolving interface issues and timing the implementation.

- The date when the problem will first affect the organisation (Often, well before January 1st, 2000)

Performing a critical systems test

A Critical Systems Test (CST) allows systems which are critical to the running of your organisation to be checked for Year 2000 compliancy. Set up a 'test' computer system that simulates your 'main' system, then run a CST on the test system.

Include a date roll-over-type test as described in Chapter 16. Performing a CST can provide four main benefits:

- Identifies weak areas or areas that require attention

- Provides important data about your systems

- Clearly identifies inadequacies

- The results of a CST can help motivate an indifferent management to take positive action

Here's one simple practical method to help convince your manager there's a Year 2000 problem on board:

1 Learn all you can about the Y2K problem.

2 Assess and determine how it will impact the organisation in concrete terms.

3 Present relevant facts, not emotive statements. Avoid introducing overblown and often hyped media-related offerings: your managers have probably seen them all before anyway.

4 Avoid using scare tactics unless they're based on facts that are relevant to the organisation.

5 Do consider using scare tactics if you can demonstrate the organisation will almost certainly be involved in litigation come 2000.

Step 2: Assessing what is required

Once the serious decision-makers in an organisation are fully aware of the Year 2000 problem and its implications, you can then establish what action needs to be taken.

It's important to find out what is affected in your organisation. Essentially, this is what step 2 does. Broadly, step 2 is really made up of two parts: (1) performing a systems inventory (2) carrying out a systems audit.

Why bother doing an inventory and audit?

The inventory should allow you to get a broad idea of the size and extent of the problem. The results of the inventory also form a basis on which to establish funding levels and other resources necessary for the essential systems audit later, and for solving the entire Y2K problem in your organisation. This approach can be just as relevant to smaller companies as larger ones – perhaps more so!

What does the systems inventory and audit cover?

The systems inventory and audit provides a picture of all computer-based hardware and software within an organisation. Typically, it needs to account for components like:

REMEMBER

One of the most important areas a systems audit should identify is the Time To Failure (TTF). Although the TTF identifies the maximum time you have to fix the Y2K problem for each application, remember different applications often work together, so the problem may be more complex than at first thought.

HANDY TIP

As with any complex task, if you plan in detail what you hope to achieve, you're more likely to achieve desired results sooner rather than later.

- Computer hardware and related peripherals
- Each BIOS type and version used in the hardware
- Range of operating systems currently used
- A list of all active computer languages
- Applications software (databases, spreadsheets, etc.)
- Other software tools like compilers, debuggers, etc.
- Data processing methods and procedures
- An assessment of the data flow into your organisation from suppliers and the data flow out of your organisation to your clients
- The Time To Failure (TTF)

...cont'd

Analysing your computer systems

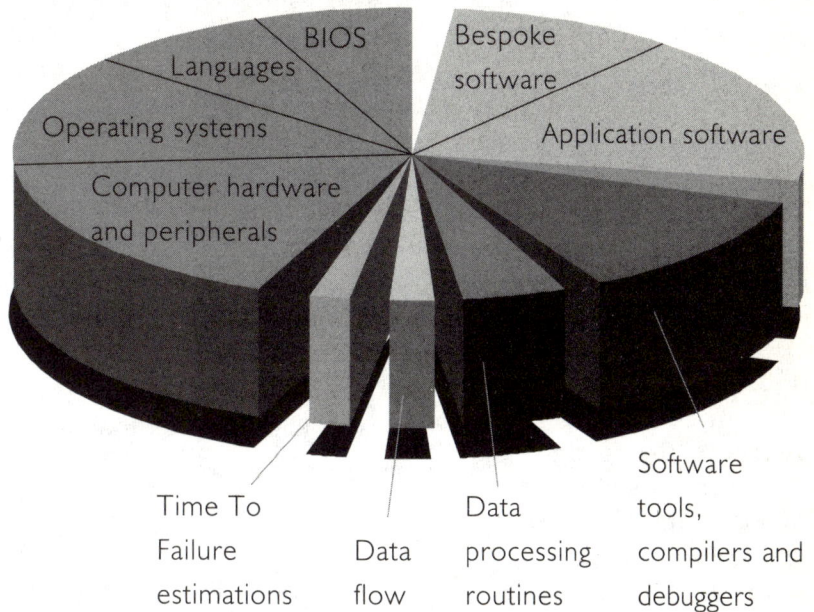

Pie chart labelled: BIOS, Languages, Bespoke software, Operating systems, Application software, Computer hardware and peripherals, Time To Failure estimations, Data flow, Data processing routines, Software tools, compilers and debuggers

REMEMBER

At first glance, carrying out step 2 in this guide may appear to provide little benefit to an organisation. However, as you'll see later, organisations can emerge from a successful Y2K repair plan as better equipped to compete in the 21st century.

The previous list is a general guide: your organisation may have more specific needs and these should be included. *Key point:* ideally, complete the systems inventory as soon as possible and establish a deadline (say within about a week). A full systems audit may take much longer.

Ensuring you allow enough time for a systems audit

Larger organisations are more likely to have a wider range and a more complex systems structure, so carrying out this step sooner rather than later is crucial. In fact, many larger companies may need six months to carry out a full inventory and audit to properly establish where the vulnerable areas lie.

Putting it all together

To help you get a clearer picture of what's involved, here's a stage-by-stage outline of step 2: *Assessing what is required:*

1 Perform a detailed inventory of all the current computer systems within your organisation (see page 79).

2 Identify the components which need fixing and create rough estimates of cost.

3 Management and relevant technical personnel should then review the results and start devising a time-allocation plan.

REMEMBER

Performing a systems audit requires a detailed examination of your computer systems. By doing this and providing an eventual fix, you can identify weak areas which perhaps you would not otherwise have known about, and can therefore make improvements that should help boost productivity and profits.

4 Establish requirements for and agree resources to carry out an audit of all computer systems within the organisation.

5 Perform a detailed systems audit to determine more accurately the nature of the problem (Time To Failure, etc.).

6 Compile the results of the systems audit into a report to determine how vulnerable the organisation is to the Y2K bug.

7 Establish more accurate estimates of how much money is required and what resources are needed to fix the problem.

What's involved in a systems audit?

A systems audit should cover several key areas. For example:

- You need to establish the type of date calculations used by each application. Often, this can be achieved by talking to expert users of the application and examining the source code and associated documentation

- Then you can establish and classify those applications that are expected to fail if not repaired

- You also need to consider the impact of data shared from your suppliers and data supplied to your customers

- The total number of Lines Of Code (LOC) in each computer system

Step 3: Creating a repair strategy

Prioritising your systems

When devising the best repair strategy, it's not a bad idea to analyse your computer systems and applications to establish a kind of urgency priority hierarchy. This might sound complex but it isn't really. In this way, you're establishing importance levels and defining the differences between what's important, what's most important and what's urgent. Here's one way to do it:

HANDY TIP

Consider whether you need to buy a Year 2000 simulator to test your systems in the Year 2000 state.

HANDY TIP

While carrying out your repairs, here's a strategy to separate two tasks which apparently must be completed at the same time: assign one an 'urgent' label, the other a 'most important' label. Then perform the most important task first.

1 First, identify which of your systems are so essential that if they were to fail, the organisation too would probably fail. Put these in the highest priority group 1.

2 Next, identify only those systems which, if they were to fail, would affect the smooth running of the organisation. Group these systems into the next priority group 2.

3 Now identify those systems that you use either on a day-to-day basis or occasionally and which are not critical to the survival or smooth running of the organisation. These form priority group 3.

4 Form priority group 4 by grouping those systems that are not essential and which you could retire if you chose to without causing much disruption to the running of the organisation.

5 Establish priority group 5 by identifying those systems that are so non-essential you don't intend to spend any time or money fixing them.

Once you have carried out steps 1–5 above, you know that priority groups 1 and 2 are the computer systems most in need of urgent repair. You can then create a time-conscious repair program to ensure all the groups you want to repair are repaired at the appropriate times.

Ideally, create a plan to enable you to check each application, applying one of the options below. You also need to consider individual time allocation and repair cost.

Dealing with non-compliant application software

When considering how to deal with application software in terms of the Year 2000 problem, six options usually become available:

- If possible, the simplest solution is to **upgrade** the application to a fully Y2K-compliant version

- Alternatively, consider **replacing** your current software with a similar millennium compliant off-the-shelf package which you can then customise to meet your needs (but make sure it's ready on time!)

BEWARE

If you upgrade your software to a later version and make customised changes, make sure these changes don't affect your new Year 2000 compliant status.

- If neither of the two above options is possible, consider **modifying your software** so that it can *process* four-digit year dates properly. This option could be favourable if (1) you have a large quantity of archived data which might otherwise have to also be checked and repaired, or (2) if you're planning to retire the application soon anyway – this usually represents the cheaper route

- A (usually) more expensive option, is to consider **repairing** the software so that it can handle the four-digit (YYYY) years properly

- **Migrate** to a different computing platform. For example, this might mean changing from say a COBOL-based system to a Client/Server Windows NT platform. However, this sort of change is a serious move and should be considered only as part of a wider overall action plan

- **Retire** the application. Sometimes, a Y2K-driven systems inventory/systems audit can identify non-essential applications and processes. If you decide to retire an application, this is one Year 2000 option that can actually save you money!

...cont'd

	1st choice: **UPGRADE**
	2nd choice: **REPLACE**

BEWARE If you decide to upgrade an off-the-shelf application, get written confirmation of Y2K-compliancy.

BEWARE If you decide to migrate to a new computing platform, make sure the software you choose is fully Year 2000 compliant.

3rd choice: **MODIFY**

Apply a logical fix

Perform an 'apparent' century repair

Install a program patch

4th choice: **REPAIR**

Carry out a 'true' four-digit century repair

5th choice: **MIGRATE**

6th choice: **RETIRE**

Often, the overall best repair solution is to use a mix of 'logical' and 'true' fixes.

Although a logical fix is a popular method of apparently repairing the symptom, it may not cure the overall problem. You need to weigh all the aspects against an urgent timescale.

Logical fixes can usually be implemented quicker, but often require in-depth and thorough testing to ensure they work properly over a range of different situations.

Repairing non-compliant software

So how do we repair the code to make it Year 2000 compliant. Four main methods exist for repairing with year 2000 non-compliant software:

- Apply a program patch: an ideal solution if you only have a 'small' Y2K problem. Patches can also sometimes be used to provide you with extra time to develop a more permanent solution

- Make an 'apparent' century repair: this approach uses wonderfully effective programming routines to give the impression that instances of two-digit year format are really four-digit format, even though no 'true' date conversion actually takes place. This technique is also known as century inferencing. Apparent repairs are ideal if you have a large amount of archived data, as this data need not be converted in the 'true' sense

- Make a 'true' repair: convert all instances of two-digit-year format to four-digit-year format

- Carry out a logical fix: this approach uses programming techniques to make a four-digit-year value fit into the space occupied by a two-digit-year value. If you use this method, both the applications and the data must be changed, ensuring that both your software applications and their associated data can be made millennium compliant

Using bridging programs

Sometimes, data formats from various different sources within your organisation are incompatible with each other. When this happens, Y2K repairers can develop bridging programs to make the necessary conversions, like for example: from two-digit-year format to four-digit-year format and back again.

Program interfaces: potential weak links

We refer to those components in a software application which accept data in and send data out as program

...cont'd

interfaces. These are like the doors of a house: if we leave them open, unlocked or unguarded, we may not know who or what is coming in or going out.

Therefore, your strategy should also include procedures and routines for dealing with data from sources outside of your organisation.

For example, if your systems were made millennium compliant, how would they handle data from suppliers who aren't Year 2000 compliant?

HANDY TIP

If you move data electronically across program interfaces, discuss the structure and rules of the interfaces early on with all those involved to ensure all parties concerned are in agreement.

And if your systems perform some procedures on your supplier-originated data, and then output the results to your customers, would the outcome provide a compliant or a non-compliant result? Errors in the interfaces could prove costly – and not just financially!

To help you tackle this area, as a rough guide, consider the following procedures:

1   If your organisation uses Electronic Data Interchange (EDI), where data is automatically moved in to and out of your computer system, acknowledge the importance of providing working interfaces beyond 2000.

2   Discuss the aspects of program interfaces with those concerned: usually your suppliers and customers

3   Realise that even if you achieve Year 2000 compliance, unless these issues are addressed your new system could be 're-infected' through these program interfaces by your suppliers and/or customers.

4   If your organisation has independently-run branches or self-governing profit centres, the amount of data throughput is likely to be much higher. Don't forget to bring these aspects into your discussions.

Setting up and using a Configuration Management System (CMS)

A CMS is a software package that enables you to make changes to software and record all the changes while maintaining the basic configuration of the original system.

An effective CMS is one of the most essential aids you can use to deal with the Year 2000 problem. Here's why using a CMS-based approach to solve your Year 2000 problem can be so valuable. A CMS:

HANDY TIP

If the complexity of your computer systems warrants it, try to set up and use a Configuration Management System (CMS) during your Y2K repair project.

BEWARE

If you use a CMS, make sure you include all the latest updates and repair changes for the final Year 2000-repaired version(s) of the software.

HANDY TIP

If the complexity of your systems warrants it, devise a test master plan to determine in depth how testing is to be carried out.

•   Allows you to make copies of the computer code while performing normal version updates and repairs

•   Once you've made a copy, you can perform day-to-day maintenance and updates while repairing the Year 2000 bug on the other copy

With a CMS, once you've completed any normal updates and included any desired version enhancements, you can copy all the Year 2000 changes/repairs to create a fully up-to-date Year 2000 compliant software version.

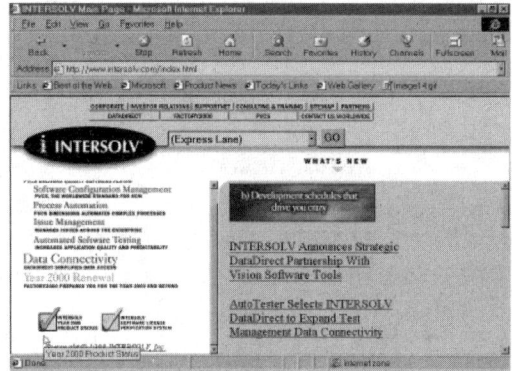

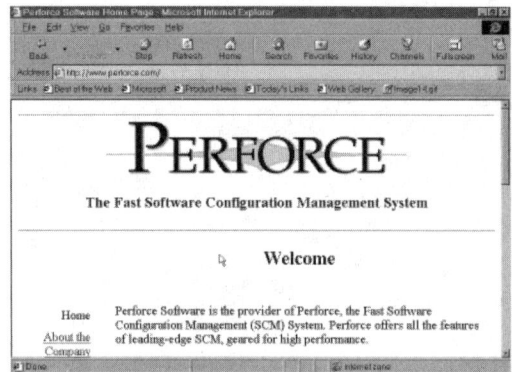

Step 4: Demonstrating how it works

Sometimes, testing should be carried out repeatedly. One of the best ways to do this is to use a test script – a list of instructions that provides an ideal way to test a series of data using a logically defined pattern.

When running a pilot test program, use a software measurement tool if possible to help establish goals at organisational, divisional, departmental and team levels.

Time spent working on a pilot system is not wasted. Pilots help lay the foundations for the main repair. Pilots also allow you to put mistakes right before they become troublesome.

This step is really all about testing your repair strategy. There area two ways in which you can do this:

- Test using a pilot simulation
- Test on your live system

Devise test strategies

Repairing the Year 2000 bug is one thing, proving that it's repaired is something else. Also, testing must often be thorough and variable to be effective. Therefore, devise a plan to ensure testing is done properly.

Ideally, an organisation should test its Y2K repair strategy at least one year before 2000, providing a year to make any corrections. However, some might argue that even one year may not allow enough time to perform thorough testing over a wide range of data!

However, no two organisations are the same and much depends on internal corporate politics, the teamwork factor and the desire across the board to achieve such an important goal. *Key point*: when survival is threatened, people can develop an amazing capacity to work together.

Test on a simulated 'pilot' system first

One of the most important points to remember is to first test your repair strategy on a simulated system, not your live working system. Then, if problems do occur and you need to make further changes to your repair strategy, at least you can continue your daily activities without interruption.

The pilot system can be essentially similar to the main system, *but the pilot should not contain any active interfaces to any outside computer systems that come under your responsibility*. The main value of a pilot system is that it can teach much about what to expect when you repair the 'main' system.

When you've noted the effects of running a pilot and made the appropriate changes, you're probably ready to run live.

Step 5: Implementing your strategy

By this time, you've: (1) decided to repair your systems, (2) identified all the different locations in the code containing dates, (3) established the best way to tackle each one. Now you're at the stage of implementing your plans.

To recap, remember we can use one or more of the following methods to repair the software:

- Apply a program patch

- Make an 'apparent' century repair

- Make a 'true' repair

- Carry out a logical fix

And we may use bridging programs to speed up the repair process.

Unit testing

Each repaired code module should also be thoroughly tested to ensure the results conform to the new conditions.

A note about the critical timing of the interfaces

Even if you could repair all of your Year 2000 systems in one go, you wouldn't want to: the disruption cost would probably be too high. But this brings us to the question of timing and how important it is.

Some systems will be more critical than others, and you must decide which to tackle first, which to leave till later, and which to leave till last. And of course you may decide some non-essential systems are simply not worth repairing or upgrading.

Every project has stress points – those stages which are particularly critical. We know that those parts of our computer systems that can 'connect' with others are particularly important – these are the program interfaces.

As far as implementation is concerned, implementing the repair strategy is probably reasonably straightforward once the technical hurdles have been overcome.

HANDY TIP The Y2K problem can swallow up a lot of time and resources. If time is running out, the development and application of bridging programs can sometimes help provide temporary (or permanent) working solutions to give you more time to develop a better solution.

HANDY TIP Routines designed to carry out 'apparent' century conversions, can often be used in a wider sense, not just for a single application. This enables you to do more with less and so, if appropriate, usually leads to cost savings.

BEWARE **Correcting one type of date processing error in one application does not usually provide an automatic guarantee that the same approach when applied to similar applications will provide the same successful result.**

One of the biggest problems will be deciding the timing of your implementation. Remember, if your systems interface (connect electronically) with others – such as suppliers and clients – you need to ensure that your timing is right for them too.

Otherwise, suddenly bringing new Y2K-repaired system online without discussion, agreement and arrangement will probably cause havoc to your suppliers and possibly clients too!

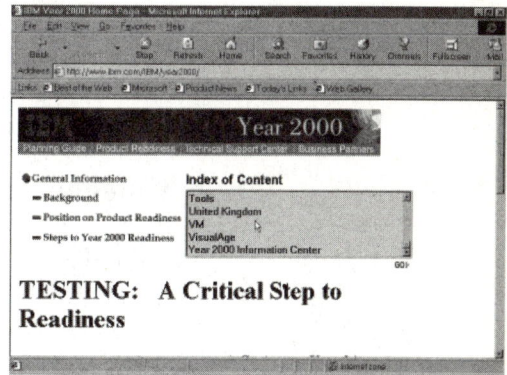

TESTING: A Critical Step to Readiness

REMEMBER **The logical fix approach, in which a four-digit year value is made to fit into the space occupied by a two-digit year value, can work well providing the data has not already been compressed.**

The ideal solution is for both you and all the parties that you connect with to upgrade and implement the new repaired system at the same time. That way, everybody concerned is synchronised.

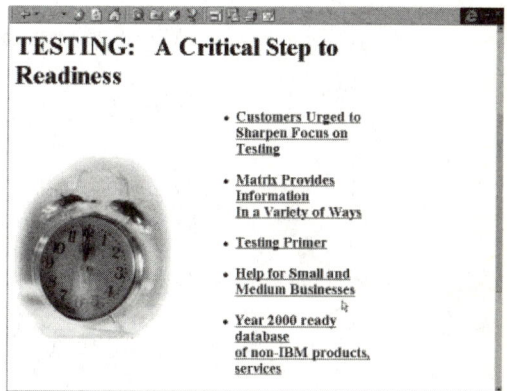

TESTING: A Critical Step to Readiness

- Customers Urged to Sharpen Focus on Testing
- Matrix Provides Information In a Variety of Ways
- Testing Primer
- Help for Small and Medium Businesses
- Year 2000 ready database of non-IBM products, services

REMEMBER **Carrying out the repairs is essentially a technical step, rather than a management-dominated activity.**

Operational testing

Once your repair is implemented, don't forget to carry out an in-depth series of operational test programs to ensure all is well when working with 'live' data.

Especially check the validity of electronic data flow between your organisation and those your computer systems interface with.

Step 6: Staying alert

By this time, you've:

- Updated or replaced your computer-base hardware if necessary

- Updated your operating systems if necessary

- Updated/repaired all relevant application software

- Dealt with the problem of dates in your data

So now you're fully millennium compliant, ready to face anything the new millennium would care to throw at you. But don't sit back and think you're safe. There's still one more step you should take on board. Essentially, at least for the next few years, this stage really isn't a step at all; rather it's a state of mind. Step 6 is really all about looking at ways in which you can prevent your Year 2000-compliant systems from being re-infected by data from outside sources.

What happens if ...

If you don't set up defence procedures, your systems could be 're-infected' at any time. And considering the insidious nature of the Year 2000 problem, you may not know you've been re-infected for some time. The longer the problem goes on of course, the more costly it is to put right. So please do consider *Step 6: Staying alert* as a genuine part of the Y2K bug remedy process.

Consider the following guidelines for step 6:

1 Make sure the procedures defined for dealing with the program interfaces are maintained.

2 Decide how you're going to deal with non-compliant dates from any outside source not yet covered.

3 Keep monitoring your defences and quickly correct any errors found. Then, change your systems to ensure the same thing doesn't happen again.

Purchasing Hardware and Software

When implementing a plan to overcome the Year 2000 problem in your company or organisation, you may decide the most cost effective option is to upgrade or purchase new computer hardware and software. This chapter tackles some of the issues you might come across and includes some essential purchasing guidelines.

Covers

Chapter Twenty

Deciding to upgrade hardware

The PC market has changed enormously during the last few years. Computer makers, quite rightly, are forever trying to look for new ways in which to make better and cheaper PCs. Often (but not always) cheaper PCs may use electronic chips from sources other than the large well known companies like Intel. This practice doesn't necessarily make a PC better or worse, it's really just economics!

HANDY TIP

If you need to upgrade or replace any computer hardware, ideally have your new compliant hardware in place by the end of 1998, to provide a margin for error if any faults develop with it.

From Chapter 2, remember that the BIOS chip in a PC holds essential date information which is also

Power Macintosh G3 Desktop

Power Macintosh G3 Minitower

PowerBook G3

usually accessed through the computer's operating system in order to set the 'system' date and time. For non-compliant BIOS chips, sometimes you may still be able to obtain an upgrade, either as a new replacement chip or as a 'flash' software upgrade.

REMEMBER

If you decide to upgrade a mother-board, sometimes you may need to update the memory chips used also. Look into this option thoroughly before committing yourself to the idea.

However, sometimes you may be unlucky and find that no compatible BIOS chip is available. So what do can you do if you find yourself in this situation? If date accuracy is critical to your work, here are some options to think about:

- You could consider upgrading the motherboard, but going down this route may have other implications (see margin). Often, in such circumstances, this could offer the cheapest upgrade path. But do learn as much as you can about the subject before attempting such a major upgrade (see Handy Tip on opposite page margin)

- Maybe the only real answer would be to buy another PC and use your current model for minor work

...cont'd

In real terms, PC prices have fallen dramatically in recent years, and there's no reason why this shouldn't continue, at least in the short term. If you do decide to purchase new hardware, consider the guidelines throughout this chapter to help you get the best deal.

See the latest Dell range on: http://www.euro.dell.com/

To find out more about Gateway's latest products, try: http://www.gw2k.co.uk/

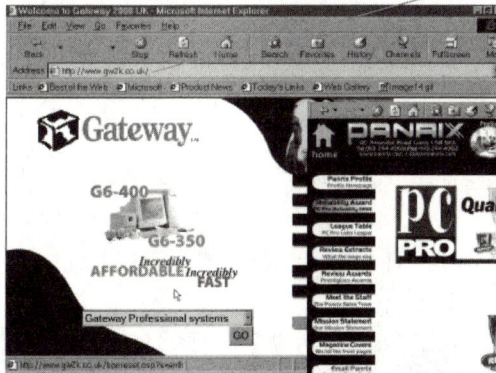

See Panrix at: http://www.panrix.co.uk/

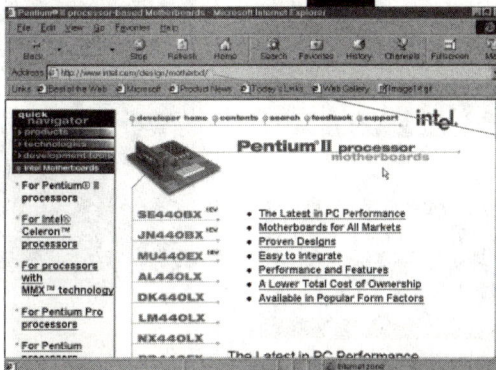

HANDY TIP

Computer Step cover this area in their book *Upgrading your PC*, from the same "in easy steps" series, available from all good book shops or direct from the publisher.

Information about Intel's motherboards is available at: http://www.intel.com

Evaluating purchase options

Arguably the best way to buy a computer system

Your computer system in some ways is like an employee: it helps you achieve what you want to achieve. However, often we tend to think of a computer simply as that (often cursed) box that sits on our desk, rather than in terms of what we want a computer to do for us. Here's one method to help you avoid making the most common mistake when buying or leasing a computer system:

When buying a computer system, don't buy the hardware first followed by the software you want. Do it the other way round: buy software first, then purchase only hardware that's capable of running your chosen software.

1 Firstly, it might seem obvious but take a few minutes to note down the main reasons why you want a computer. These could include: word processing, desktop publishing, working with spreadsheets, databases, surfing the Internet, email, etc.

2 The answers defined in step 1 above greatly influence your software choices. Remember, it's the software that creates the results for you: the computer hardware is really only a 'container' for the software. Choose your software by considering the guidelines in step 3.

Shareware is essentially a try-before-you-buy system of purchasing computer software.

3 Make a list of the things you want the software to do. Label the most important thing number 1, the next most important, number 2, and so on.

...cont'd

4 When you're ready to buy the software, shop around. Talk to computer dealers. Try to secure the best deal. Read the reviews in computer magazines – they can reduce the risk for you, but ultimately make your own choice. Don't forget to consider shareware software. Talk to friends and colleagues and try out the software or see a demonstration before you buy and don't forget, it must be Year 2000 compliant.

   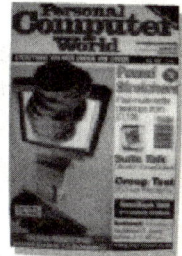

5 Then buy your hardware. Also, get written guarantees that your chosen hardware is Year 2000 compliant.

Shareware has now come of age. Most shareware software is as stable as its commercial counterparts (sometimes more so). A wide range of excellent products are available and often cost much less than you might have thought.

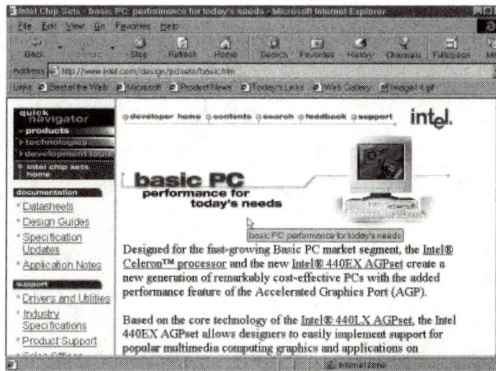

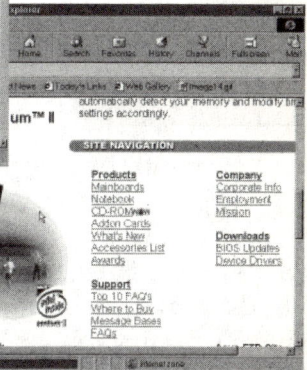

Some purchasing power tips

You can buy, rent or lease computers. Each option has its own merits and drawbacks. Sometimes it pays to consider a different option.

If your computer needs involve spending a considerable sum of money, and if you're not familiar with computer systems, you could benefit by discussing your needs with a reputable computer consultant. Sometimes, they can secure discounts from sources you haven't considered.

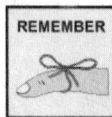

When purchasing hardware, don't forget your future needs: make sure there's plenty of expansion potential possible.

The in-store Year 2000 compliancy test

Here's one simple but powerful tip to save you much time and hassle if you decide to buy from a computer store. If you want to be 100% sure that both your hardware and any software you're buying is Year 2000 compliant, insist on carrying out an in-store test for Year 2000 compliancy.

Most reasonable retailers will understand a buyer's sensitivity over the Year 2000 issue: there's been a lot of media coverage and when you're spending a lot of hard earned cash, it's not a lot to ask. Some forward-looking stores even have their own Year 2000 test procedures ready to run for customers, but they may not bother to unless you ask.

This way, you can check the hardware, operating system and any application software in one go. And know that come January 1st, 2000, you're not going to develop a Year 2000 headache for the rest of the week!

Buying computer hardware

Computer hardware essentially covers two things: the computers themselves and the peripherals like printers, scanners, and so forth.

Computer hardware comes in a variety of appearances nowadays including: high power minicomputers, servers, desktop PCs, notebooks, Apple Macs, the smaller Psion 5-type devices and those based on the Windows CE operating system. Consider the following buying tips:

1. Purchase, lease or rent the most powerful hardware you can afford! For Desktop and notebook PCs, include at least 64Mb of RAM. Ideally, aim for a minimum of 128 Mb of RAM.

2. Often PCs come with a range of bundled software. If you don't want or need this, try to secure a discount. You may secure a further discount by offering cash instead of credit card, but remember, you don't usually have the same level of consumer protection if things go wrong.

There's a wide choice of top names on the Web

REMEMBER

Computers and software have high resale values. Put in place procedures to cover their security. *Securing your data and systems* **in Chapter 3 provides some ideas to consider.**

REMEMBER

When buying new computer systems, don't forget to consider service support and breakdown packages if required. Some products even come with free lifetime support. Check into these details at the time of purchase to secure the best deals.

Buying a second-hand computer

You may wonder why we decided to include this section. After all, buying complex electronic equipment is a risky business, right? Answer: yes and no. Consider the following observations:

- If you're unlucky enough to have a fault with a new computer, the chances are it will happen within 4–6 weeks of the date of purchase. After the initial period, things seem to settle down and reliability improves

- A new computer is always going to be the best option simply because it's new, probably fast, and often includes a bundle of software (although, you may not use most of it regularly!)

- A new computer can loose up to 50% of its value within the first month

- After one year has elapsed, it loses another 10–20% of its original value

HANDY TIP

When evaluating a used computer, you can save time and ensure the computer you're interested in is Y2K compliant by running a Y2K-checking utility, at the time of purchase. Some freeware utilities are listed on pages 163 and 164.

Now, here's the big one: buy a computer which is about a year old and you could provide yourself with an excellent deal in terms of reliability in relation to cost. Also, if you buy from a reputable computer dealer, often you can secure a three-month guarantee. From results of the author's own experience and research, IBM, Compaq and Dell desktop PCs are always worth considering. For laptops, Toshiba are particularly well known for their reliability.

There are also many more good makes that we simply haven't got the space to mention, so if you can, speak to work colleagues, friends and acquaintances to find out their experiences with using different computers.

Make sure it's compliant

If you decide to buy a second-hand computer, don't forget: one of the most important points to check is that it is compliant. Get a written pledge that your chosen PC is Y2K compliant. Ideally, run a test to prove it at the time of purchase (see pages 163–164 for free testing software).

The Sale of Goods Act 1979

This is one area in which a little knowledge could save you a lot of money. And if you live outside of the UK, the chances are that your country has similar laws to protect the buyer from unfair practices.

We're not suggesting that computer vendors are unfair or unscrupulous: the vast majority are only too willing to help their customers whenever they can – after all, this is good business sense. However, you may come across the odd few who may try to avoid their responsibilities for whatever reason. If this is your situation, here's what you should know.

Software purchased in the UK within the last couple of years should be millennium compliant. If it isn't, you could argue quite reasonably that it's not 'fit for the purpose for which it is intended', as defined in the UK Sale of Goods Act of 1979.

Non-compliant software purchased recently

If you purchased software from say 1996/7 that you later discover is not Year 2000 compliant, contact your supplier, developer or software manufacturer. Under these conditions, it's not unreasonable to expect a free Year 2000 repair upgrade.

Considering the date you purchased the software, arguably the software manufacturer should have addressed the Year 2000 problem at that time. This argument is stronger if the software you purchased is specialised and therefore particularly expensive.

Arguing that a purchase of this nature comes under the Sale of Goods Act may not be easy. However, the mere mention of consumer laws can often bring swift results and so is certainly worth trying. Also, some thrifty organisations may decide to provide upgrades only to those customers who demonstrate that they're more informed than most! You read it here first.

REMEMBER

If you live outside the UK, check out the laws in your own country designed to protect the buyer from unfair practices.

HANDY TIP

Some organisations may simply not want the kind of 'exposure' of finding out their true level of legal obligation. Being firm but polite may help produce the desired result.

Trouble with recent purchases?

If you're unhappy with the lack of Year 2000 compliance, contact your supplier as soon as possible and discuss your grievances. Be open-minded and try to see things from their point of view, but don't be fobbed off with lame excuses. If necessary, put your grievances in writing. Keep all records related to the purchase of your hardware or software. Record the dates of all relevant telephone calls and meetings, and what was discussed.

Be reasonable: if the hardware or software is four or more years old, your demand will probably not be considered valid. However, if the problem is relatively easy to correct, some companies and organisations may offer to put matters right in the interests of good customer relations – especially if you have a good past record of doing business with them. These companies are usually the ones that we'll see grow in the 21st century!

How the Internet can help you

Sometimes, a polite, to-the-point letter to the highest authority in the organisation may be required. If you think an organisation is being particularly unfair, by all means seek expert legal advice.

Alternatively, one low-cost method which may be particularly effective is to mention your easy access to, and effective use of, the Internet: it would be simple to relate your story to millions across the globe using a variety of legal means. However, if you do actually use the Internet in this way, be very careful: you may need to spend some of your hard-earned leisure time devising how to relate your story without falling foul of legal ramifications, because how you word such material is very important. Otherwise you could end up in court defending a slander or libel case!

When faced with the possibility of their good name being bandied about the Web or sullied on the Internet newsgroups, most organisations who know that they're really in the wrong would probably want to rectify the situation, or at least make a conciliatory gesture. If so, listen and be flexible. Try to come to an agreement.

Year 2000 Problem-solving Resources

Apart from the obvious Year 2000 resources, there are others providing vital information – often available for free. Central to these are the Internet and the Web. In this chapter, we show you what's available and how you can use these valuable resources to help keep you abreast of the latest developments.

Covers

Consulting organisations

Earlier in this book, we mentioned at what first glance might seem a rather unusual fact: larger organisations, even with all the extra resources they can muster, usually have a larger Year 2000 problem than their smaller counterparts.

Even with a full IT support department, most of the people working on the problem will probably already be stretched: Often, there's just not enough spare time during the working day (or night) to get everything done. Many people may already be suffering severe stress-related symptoms and all that they bring. These events simply make the problem even bigger.

Getting extra help

Many of the larger organisations already have consulting organisations working hard trying to solve their clients' problems. There are literally thousands of Y2K consulting organisations available.

Here's a list containing some useful contacts in the UK. Provision of the following list is not necessarily an endorsement or recommendation: we simply wanted to give you a starting point:

- Implement Limited. Web address:
  http://www.implement.co.uk/index.htm
  Tel: + 44 (0)1442 251534, Fax: + 44 (0)1442 213226.
  Email: *sales@implement.co.uk*

- Elmbronze Limited. Web address:
  http://www.elmbronze.demon.co.uk/year2000/
  Email: *year2000@elmbronze.demon.co.uk*

- Durham Systems Management Limited. Web address:
  http://www.year2000.co.uk/mainfram.htm
  Email: *sheila@year2000.co.uk*

- Greenwich 2000 Limited. Web address:
  http://millennium.greenwich2000.com/
  millennium/year2000/index.htm
  Email: *sales@greenwich2000.com*

PC Year 2000 testers & repairers

Here's a list of useful programs that include combined Year 2000 testing and fix utilities:

Testing standalone PCs

With shareware, you have a license to try the product and if you decide to use it, you're obliged to pay the usually very reasonable fee to the software author.

- **Correx 2000 v1.1** tests for the Year 2000 problem. It also provides an alternative to that of a BIOS update by using a Terminate and Stay Resident (TSR) fix approach instead. A TSR device driver is a small software program that's loaded each time you switch on your PC. *Correx 2000* is for checking standalone products so it can't check a network. For more information, call Secure PC on: + 44 (0)171 610 3646, or fax: + 44 (0)171 610 3484. At the time of writing *Correx 2000* costs £49.95 plus VAT

Freeware items cost nothing, but do consider reading the originator's mailers or log on to their Web site as a form of repayment if you're asked.

- **Y2K** – is a small, plain and simple MS-DOS/PC-DOS-based shareware product that tests for Y2K errors in your computer's RTC clock/BIOS/operating system. *Y2K* can make the date changes for you, tell you what it's doing and when the tests are complete, it resets your date and time back to your original settings. *Y2K* doesn't test application software or data: both of these should be checked on a case-by-case basis. At the time of writing, it costs only £10 sterling or $15 US dollars. You can obtain a copy from Web address: *http://waverlyweb.com* or send an email to: help@waverlyweb.com or fax: + 44 (0)1428 685544 or phone: + 44 (0)1428 685533

- **NSTL Ymark** is an ideal software utility that also checks a standalone PC, so it's not designed for testing a network. *NSTL Ymark is* freeware, so you don't need to pay. There's no technical support, but it's easy to use anyway and FAQ sheets are available on the Web site. You can download a copy from: *http://www.nstl.com* To use it, first double-click on the file you downloaded – Y2000.exe. This creates two more files: a text file and 2000.exe – the test utility. Next, at the DOS prompt, move to the directory containing 2000.exe, then type: 2000.exe and follow onscreen instructions

Testing a network

- **Span 2000** can test standalone PCs or an entire network for Year 2000-related problems using network log-in scripts. Although designed to run from a DOS platform, it can still be run from PCs containing Windows 3.XX and Windows 95/98. *Span 2000* costs £195 plus VAT at the time of writing. For more information, point your Web browser at: *http://www.span2000.com/* or call: + 44 (0)800 897695 or fax: + 44 (0)800 897638

- **Centennial 2000 Enterprise Edition** offers a relatively simple way to test networked and standalone PCs for Year 2000 compliance. Using Windows 95 or NT, you can determine the Y2K position of every PC on your network. *Centennial* supports NetWare, Windows NT and IntranetWare network operating systems. The software can also control the installation of Flash BIOS upgrades from its Control Centre. Cost at the time of writing is £280 plus VAT for a 10-user licence. For more information, call: + 44 (0)1488 882444 or fax: + 44 (0)1488 682429 or point your Web browser at: *http://www. centennial.co.uk/*

Automatically repairing some non-compliant PCs

- **Holmesfx** is a valuable freeware utility that automatically sets the date on a PC which doesn't move over to the next century dates properly. *Holmesfx* is not a Terminate and Stay Resident (TSR) program, but rather installs some changes on to your AUTOEXEC.BAT file – one of your PC's 'start-up' files. One limitation: this program can't put right the BIOSes that you've tried to set manually but which failed. You can download a copy from: *http://www.wsnet.com/~designer/holmesfx/*

    As a point of interest: note the tilde (~) symbol in the Web address above. To type this character, simply press and hold down the SHIFT key while you press the #(hash) key.

Year 2000 problem-solving tools

Here's a general list of categories of tools available that are ideal in helping companies and organisations ease the burden of Year 2000 repair:

BEWARE Year 2000 software tools can help ease the burden of repair/conversion and can save much time. However, don't rely totally on *any* tools. Year 2000 repairs must be checked by people who have a real understanding of the implications and what is required.

REMEMBER If you decide to use any of these tools, as with any new software, you need time to learn to use them. This is often a vastly underestimated cost. Build a realistic allowance for training time into your costing budgets.

Software inventory tools

Programs can come in a variety of types and many organisations are continually adding modules, updates, commands, and so on. Software inventory tools can help identify all the programs in a computer system and help you gain a better understanding of what is required for an effective and successful Year 2000 repair.

Costing the Year 2000 repair project

Estimating how much it's all going to cost is often a tricky undertaking. However, tools are available to help you forecast and manage the entire project.

Configuration Management System (CMS) tools

CMS tools help provide a disciplined approach and formal control over recording and tracking Year 2000 repairs and conversions. Software version changes can be logged and monitored through to final repair/conversion. Many Year 2000 experts consider CMS tools to be essential for dealing with a 'large' Year 2000 problem.

However, do remember if you decide to use CMS software, these tools also use dates, so make sure the tool you choose does not itself have any Year 2000-related problems.

Year 2000 renovation/conversion tools

Two-digit year date references are central to the Year 2000 problem. You can speed up the job of identification and repair by using special tools to identify all two-digit year date references.

Impact analysis

These tools allow you to assess the impact of making Year 2000 changes. Often, it's essential to understand in more depth the real effects of making changes to your systems before you make them and to determine how these changes affect routines between programs and across different computer systems.

Software reverse engineering tools

These tools are useful to help gain a better understanding of how a program works and to also help identify 'dead' code – that is code that has not been used for years and which can be deleted without causing problems to your current computer systems.

Year 2000 test simulators

These can be useful to allow testing to be carried out on your systems in the Year 2000 state. These tools usually work by providing a simulated system clock to run applications through the 'hot' year 2000-related dates.

Year 2000 test and validation tools

Carrying out Year 2000 repairs is one thing; making sure the repairs are valid, and work correctly over the entire range of target data types and computer systems, is something else.

> **HANDY TIP**
>
> **Some software tools that need to be purchased to carry out Year 2000 repairs properly, may also be useful for other projects later on. Code analysers and database converters are two such examples.**

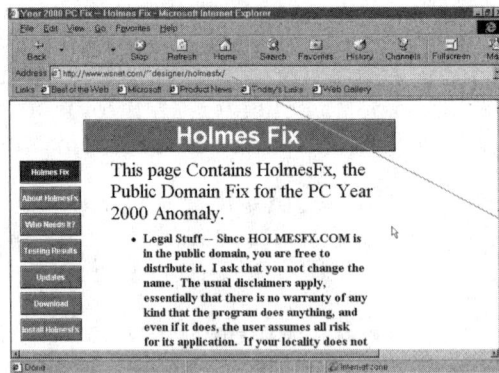

This freeware utility can automatically adjust the date on PCs that don't roll over properly on December 31st, 1999. View it at: http://www.wsnet. com/~designer/holmesfx/

Tools that help with testing can be invaluable, as thorough testing is such an important step in beating the bug. Typical examples of these tools can work at unit, system and Year 2000 integration levels. Validation tools can help demonstrate the validity of Year 2000 fixes across a wide range of systems.

Key Year 2000 data on the Internet

The Internet and Web represent two valuable resources for anyone wanting to find out more about the Year 2000 problem. Many Web sites are now highlighting a range of different issues. Of course, many of these organisations have a vested interest in doing so. But one thing is certain: if they mention urgency, they're not wrong.

Useful Year 2000 sources on the Web

The World Wide Web (WWW) is particularly valuable when you want to find out information about the Year 2000 problem. If you're wanting to find out more information generally, try using the search engines as examined in: *Searching the Internet* later in this section.

If you want to see specific sites, consider the following:

REMEMBER **By the time this book is in print, your local bookshop may stock a range of books covering the Year 2000 bug. However, one reason why the author wrote this book was that he found this wasn't the case in the UK, even in 1997.**

- **Taskforce 2000** was set up some time ago to provide information and advice to companies and organisations. Web address at: *http://www.taskforce2000.co.uk/*

- **Action 2000** includes strong support for small- to medium-sized organisations. Phone: + 44 (0)845 601 2000. Web site address: *http://www.open.gov.uk/bug2000/*

- **The Central Computer and Telecommunications Agency (CCTA)** for advice and information. Web site address: *http://www.open.gov.uk/mill/mbhome.htm*

- **ComplY2K** provides organisations with an in-depth analysis of their Y2K problem and a strategy to fix it. Web address: **http://www.comply2k.com/**

- **BugNet** is a collaboration of interested parties, government organisations and industrial contributors that share information and relevant Web site addresses: **http://www.open.gov.uk/bug2000/**

- **The European Commission (EC)**. For information on how the Y2K problem is affected by the Euro. Web address: *http://www.ispo.cec.be/y2keuro/*

- If you're involved in a small business in the UK, you can obtain lots of useful advice from **The Year 2000 Support Centre**. Their phone and fax details are listed in the margin on page 105. Their web site is at: *http://www.support2000.com*

- **The Year 2000 Problem** site is maintained by Durham Systems Management Ltd and includes essential information and an index of other related Web links. Go to: *http://www.year2000.co.uk/*

> **BEWARE**
>
> **A wide range of more expensive books and videos are available from Internet- and Web-related sources. However, these may be particularly expensive and sometimes it's difficult to gauge whether the contents really address the issues you're interested in. Key point: ask for a preview before buying.**

- **The Year 2000 Information Centre**. Peter de Jager – the renowned and respected Year 2000 expert – has set up this *excellent* Year 2000 resource. Web address: *http://www.year2000.com/*

- If you use CompuServe, don't forget **The Year 2000** forum. It contains much useful information on year 2000 issues and makes available valuable files and discussion excerpts. To access the forum, enter *GO YEAR2000* in your CompuServe software

- **The Microsoft Year 2000 Resource Centre** provides relevant information and advice about Microsoft products, which ones are compliant – and to what level – and which aren't; plus lots of other useful data. Web address: *http://www.microsoft.com/year2000/*

- **The Y2K Support Centre** site from The Computer Information Centre. Includes a wide range of key links. Go to: *http://www.compinfo.co.uk/y2k.htm*

- The **British Standards Institute**. Includes guidelines for addressing the Year 2000 problem. Web address: *http://www.bsi.org.uk/disc/year2000.html*

- The **Year 2000 Related Links page**. From de Jager & Company Limited and The Tenagra Corporation. Includes many valuable Y2K-related links. Go to: http://www.year2000.com/links.html

- The **Unisys Web site** is dedicated to Year 2000 issues. Web address: *http://www.unisys.com/marketplace/year2000/*

- You can gain access to the **American National Standards Institute (ANSI) and the International Organisation for Standardisation (ISO) Web sites.** You can then obtain details about how computers should represent date information. Web address: *http://www.ansi.org and http://www.iso.ch*

Internet Newsgroups

- In the Usenet newsgroups, try: *comp.software.year-2000*

Searching the Internet

Many articles have already been written highlighting the Year 2000 problem, both in print and online on the Internet. You can get an idea by entering the phrase: 'Year 2000 problem'. In April 1997, the author performed this same exercise using the Alta Vista search engine and found over 4.5 million English references!

Try entering other related words and phrases, like 'Y2K problem', 'Year 2000 bug', 'Millennium bomb', and so on, to possibly identify other useful information sources and advice.

Internet ezines

Year 2000 issues are also covered in Web ezines – these are email-based magazines. Try:

- **Com.Links** Magazine. Although it has a US flavour, it contains lots of key information and the latest news and developments. Web address: *http://www.comlinks.com*

- IBM's 180-page **Year 2000 guide** is available to help users, vendors and customers perform Year 2000 repairs successfully. Web address: *http://www.software.ibm.com/year2000/ resource.html*

Don't forget the mailing lists

Here are details covering two of the most valuable Year 2000-related mailing lists available from anywhere across the globe:

- **Peter de Jager** provides one of the best sources on the Year 2000 problem on the Internet (his Web site is available on http://www.year2000.com/). He also provides a mailing list which includes a wide range of support information. If you find the list valuable, a small voluntary donation may be asked for.

  To subscribe to the list, simply send an email to *listmanager@hookup.com* and in the body of the message (not the subject box), type: SUBSCRIBE YEAR2000

  If you want to receive an abridged version of the above, send an email to the same address inserting DIGEST YEAR2000 in the body of the message

  Alternatively, send an email to: *y2k@tor.hookup.net* and enter the word SUBSCRIBE in the subject line of the message

- **Robert Arnold's Year 2000 News**. From this newsletter, you can receive a lot of useful information monthly. Currently there's no charge, but the information is copyrighted so do contact the publishers if you want to use any content. Although the publishers are keen to expand the distribution, they also like to know where the newsletter's going, so if you want to forward the newsletter to other parties, please contact Robert Arnold's people first.

  The email address is: news2000@cais.com To access Robert Arnold's email news, do this: (1) Type the message SUBSCRIBE in the subject line of your email software, (2) Then send the message to: *news2000-request@andrew.cais.com*

Chapter Twenty-two

Thinking the Unthinkable: Starting Afresh

There may be instances in which the Year 2000 problem is so entrenched and so costly to put right that it's simply not worth the hassle. In this event, perhaps a new kind of thinking is called for. The Chinese have an ideogram for crisis which also means opportunity. You could turn the potential traumas of the Year 2000 problem into a new opportunity in which you can start again with a new IT infrastructure that will be leagues ahead of your competitors. This chapter explores this revolutionary approach.

Covers

Using Y2K as a new opportunity

This chapter is all about exploring a new approach to the Year 2000 bug and all the potential problems it can bring. Here, we look at the unthinkable in terms of normal business solutions. We show that there may be some instances in which the unthinkable becomes not only possible but preferable.

Here are three benefits of starting again making maximum use of the new information technologies:

- This approach offers a completely new strategy and new tools, not a patch-up of the past

- You won't need to waste money propping up possibly outdated software and hardware

- You'll be free of the stranglehold held by a limited number of experts whose fee rates may possibly increase greatly the closer we approach year 2000

REMEMBER

If you decide to start again with a new IT infrastructure, you're leagues ahead of anyone starting a new business from scratch as you simply move your most valuable resource – your hard earned client list – to the new IT infrastructure.

But there are drawbacks, including:

- Buying into new technology is relatively expensive in the short term, even with the current trend of plunging PC costs

- And there are always going to be the perhaps often underestimated costs, like learning to use the new hardware and software

- Changing to anything new always brings with it a degree of disruption. The bigger the change, the more disruption there's likely to be

- The experience can be painful

- There's always the risk of unforeseen elements not being accounted for

- Sometimes it requires careful long-term planning; for some organisations, there isn't much time left available to create a smooth transition using this approach

The pain of starting from scratch

HANDY TIP

Most Web sites are not yet profitable. Key point: you don't have to have an all-singing-all dancing Web site to make it pay. Often, the most successful Internet marketeers make effective use some of the cheapest methods: email, 'plain' Web sites, and use of the Newsgroups.

REMEMBER

Bigger, better, more 'colourful' Web sites don't automatically mean bigger, better profits.

HANDY TIP

To market successfully on the Internet, learn all you can about the subject. Use the search engines to find key data and avoid the mistakes of others who didn't.

For some businesses and organisations, becoming Year 2000 compliant may involve much disruption and in-depth repair work.

For others, the reverse may be true: you may have found that a little creative thinking has resulted in a startling discovery – the realisation that moving operations to a new IT platform may not be as difficult as you first thought.

From new baby to athlete in a few weeks

Let's briefly explore the possibility of starting anew; is it so impossible? Imagine your organisation is relatively small, providing full-time employment for 10–20 people. Remember, three of your most important resources are brand identity, your established client base and top quality, dedicated staff. Arguably, the remaining assets are just 'bricks and mortar' and other 'replaceable' entities.

Your entire data bank is backed up daily using something like an Iomega Jaz-based disk/cartridge system. You compare the costs of fixing your Year 2000 problem with moving to a new IT platform and discover that even if you have to re-enter all your data into the new format, there's only a 10–20 per cent difference.

The benefits of updating are clear. If you decide to go this route, of course the first few weeks of the 'new' system will probably involve a steep learning curve.

But like any new birth, starting again from scratch may be both exciting and painful. After that initial conversion period however, you'll probably emerge in a much stronger business position to service your existing clients and gain new, more profitable clients quicker.

Your new thinking may include more emphasis on things like 'How can we make better and more profitable use of the Internet', as you realise how much money you may have been losing by not marketing here correctly. You realise the big secret: effective marketing on the Internet does not have to cost much (see Handy Tip in margin).

The stranglehold of the Y2K experts

Any business or organisation still with an untreated Year 2000 problem in the final quarter of 1999 will probably have to pay a great deal of money to their chosen Year 2000 consultants and repairers to rectify their problem. As the end of the millennium draws closer, fee rates will probably go higher, and higher and higher.

And we have to put our total trust in whoever we have appointed to cure the problem. How do we know the project won't drag on and on? The short answer is we simply don't and can't know these eventualities, whatever assurances are given. Any already astronomical estimates and quotations could go even higher.

The business of espionage

Often, the larger an organisation is, the greater the value of its information. Certainly, amongst the world's top players, certain information about competitors is a highly sought after commodity. And of course, smaller companies may also hold particularly valuable information contained within application code and data. Industrial espionage could also could play a part in the wheeling and dealing that goes on between large companies and their competitors.

In the context of the Year 2000 problem, it's not hard to think that some disreputable Year 2000 repair bodies may be tempted to extend and increase repair costs to one company, while also being paid by another to supply information. Thinking the unthinkable helps you to avoid falling foul of these 'unsavoury' practices.

Back to basics: re-inventing yourself

Developing new ways of thinking

Many companies and organisations could benefit from a completely new management approach and culture. Perhaps the Y2K problem can help those organisations 'get ahead of the game before it's even begun'.

What do we mean by that? Working practices are developing and changing all the time. Organisations may now have an opportunity to re-examine their approaches right across the board and think up new, better ways of working even before anyone else. Those brave pioneers could start a 'trend' that may inadvertently

HANDY TIP

Although the Year 2000 problem is a BIG headache for most organisations, for some, the inevitable build up of negativity can provide a springboard to a complete rethink that under normal circumstances you might never have even considered.

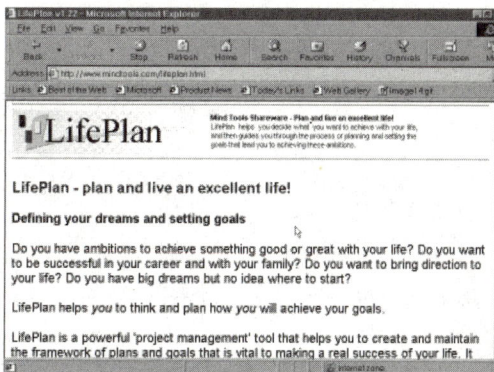

generate income they hadn't even thought of: think patents, copyright, lecture tours, and so on.

Turning the so-called crazy ideas into gold

The Year 2000 problems are an ideal forum for brainstorming new approaches, new techniques and new systems; for spending some time thinking laterally;

following up so called 'wacky ideas' that may have been trying to gain our attention, sitting in the backs of our minds perhaps for ages, if we only had the time and desire to stop, listen and explore the territory.

Rethinking the way you do business

If, as a result of the Y2K problem, we decide to reshape our thinking, ideally we want to create a new system path that ensures we can maintain valuable business advantages over our competitors.

Knowing what we know now and learning the lessons of past mistakes are one powerful stimulus when asking ourselves how would we do things if we were starting afresh. Here's some things to consider:

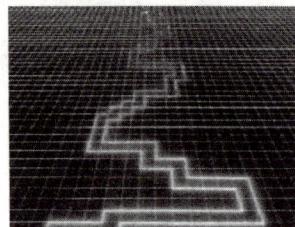

- Assess the benefits and drawbacks of adopting more flexible work strategies

- Investigate how the latest technology using modern systems thinking can help achieve more with less

- Remote working; what are the real implications?

- How to make effective use of the Internet and Web

- How to really benefit from plunging PC costs

- How the new computer networks puts company-wide power on the desktop, anywhere, any place

How big business have realised small is best!

Results of recent studies of some of the world's most effective business leaders has suggested that leaders of big businesses and institutions should start to think like small business entrepreneurs, if they have any hope of succeeding into the 21st century. For example:

- Creating better quality customer relations: greater attention to detail and provision of wider choices

- Developing customer-driven marketing campaigns

- Examining ways to improve financial performance

- How to improve staff management and motivation while learning to 'distance manage' employees

REMEMBER

Teleworking, telecommuting, remote working all refer to ways of completing work at one site and sending it using computing and telephone technology to another site.

HANDY TIP

If you're based in the UK and need to borrow money from the banks to re-finance your business, consider contacting the European Investment Bank. Why? Currently, lending rates may be several percent cheaper than the UK.

Adopting flexible work strategies

Harness the growing trend to redefine 'office space'

Currently, nearly a quarter of the UK population now perform some work at home. By 2010, some believe this figure will reach half. Clearly, there are savings to be made here. However, there are other implications: for example, those who work from home ideally need a defined work area and the discipline to avoid procrastinating and getting sidetracked by things that aren't really relevant to the day's work-related tasks.

When smaller may mean better

By harnessing new technology into core business activities, in the coming years smaller companies and organisations may be in a position to compete on a more equal footing to that of the large corporations. *The key may be found in effective use of the new technologies and knowing how to best use them in the context of your operations.*

Essential point: smaller organisations can be leaner, fitter and more flexible than their larger competitors.

Mitel have recently completed some research into technology and smaller organisations. In their report, they believe that by 2008, 2.5–4 million people in the UK will probably work from home.

Even many of the movers and shakers in the larger organisations have realised the value of smallness, by contributing to the growing trend of establishing smaller, self-governing 'profit' centres. In these, often more emphasis is put on people issues and adopting flexible work strategies to help motivate staff to improve results.

The business of remote working

If you use a PC for your work, now you no longer need to be present 'at' your traditional work location to connect with your work colleagues or your office network. As an individual working 'remotely', you can connect to anyone else who uses a computer or to the office network utilising either one of two main methods:

- Using a modem, a standard telephone line and relevant access software. Current modem speeds offer a maximum of 56 Kbits per second data transfer (one direction)

HANDY TIP

Many email systems now allow you to transfer large accompanying files as 'attachments'. Learn about email and how greater use can help save money.

- Or use a much faster ISDN adapter, ISDN telephone line and ISDN access software. However, remember that your target recipient must also be set up to receive ISDN-based information

Whatever method you choose, once connected to your network you can gain access to all the shared facilities that are available when you're actually present at the network site. For example, you can examine the group scheduler/diary, receive and respond to your email, and move and copy files between your PC and those on the network.

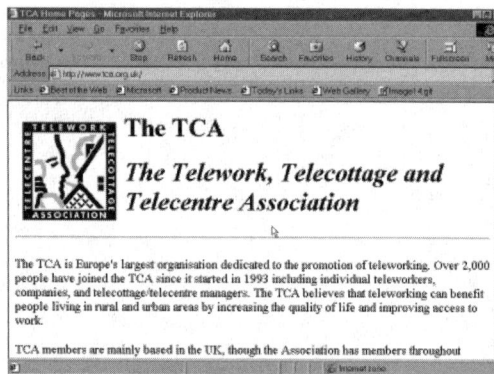

If more than one person wants to connect to the network at the same time, you'll need to install further modems at the office.

Weighing up the pros and cons

To telework essentially means much less commuting, no more time spent stuck in traffic jams, greater control over your work output and often the opportunity to work outside 'normal' office hours. Often, a quiet, uninterrupted session away from a 'busy' office environment, can provide an ideal way to achieve more with less.

However, you still need to put aside office space; consider the needs of other family members; the impact of children during school holidays, etc. And there's greater risk of feeling isolated. However, usually the savings outweigh the costs provided an employee can maintain the self discipline to accomplish the tasks in hand.

REMEMBER **A 'virtual company' is an organisation that selects and drops resources according to what's required at the time. Where these resources are sited is not relevant. This is achieved largely through the use of computer technology. British Telecom suggests that virtual companies will probably form the largest group by 2010.**

For information about telecommuting or teleworking, point your browser at: http://www.tca.org.uk/ or telephone: + 44 (0)800 616008

Pressing the trigger

For years, people have predicted the widespread take up of teleworking methods in the UK. But in practice, it simply hasn't happened. In some countries – Sweden and USA for example – teleworking is now accepted as a valid way of working, with the consequent reduction in time wastage, pollution, stress and so on, also being recognised.

History has shown that momentous changes often require a trigger event or series of events. For some organisations, the Year 2000 problem may provide such a trigger.

The combination of a growing, demand-driven Internet and the choice of ever more powerful networking computer tools that allow us to get more done in less time with fewer people, can present enormous benefits to those organisations that recognise the value of these opportunities and focus them to achieve their aims.

Benefits of the latest technologies

Fax, email and Internet access are three of the most amazing technologies to sweep across the planet. From these three, other emerging technologies will soon follow: like phone video, 3D video, and so on. Internet and Web benefits are examined in more detail on pages 184 to 186.

Harnessing the power of email

Electronic mail or email for short allows anyone to send messages without using paper. Nowadays, you don't even need to have access to a PC to send email: all sorts of other methods are emerging from mobile phones through to the use of emerging set-top television boxes.

BEWARE

Computer networks represent one of the most efficient ways possible of spreading non-compliant data. Once this kind of data invades your systems, all devices attached to the network can be considered infected. Establish methods that prevent 'bad' data being accepted by your computer systems.

You can send an email to an individual, selected individuals or any/all users on an internal network, provided they already have an email address. Received emails can be replied to immediately, printed, copied, forwarded, filed for future reference or deleted. Emails can be sent as you enter them or saved and sent later. Emails are also now often accepted as legal documentary evidence.

Accessing email on a network

If you're working at an office that has an internal computer network, you can elect to receive emails as they are sent to you. Working from your home base or other remote office space, you can easily retrieve your emails once you've connected to the company network through your modem or ISDN link.

Using a once-in-a-lifetime opportunity

IT now plays a major part of the infrastructure in any successful company or organisation. Harnessing the power of the Internet and World Wide Web *now*, instead of three, four or five years time, can provide powerful competitive advantages and benefits to any individual or organisation.

In 1998/99, we're now at the birth of the 'real' Internet. In two to four years time, many more organisations across the globe will also have realised the immense value the Internet can provide and *the competitive advantage that is available now* will have gone.

Using the new computer networks

Any network at its most basic is simply a collection of interconnected computers. The new computer networks becoming available now are revolutionizing the way we work and can perform amazing feats with information.

HANDY TIP **In a computer network, a number of CD-ROM drives can often be added to a server that has a 'tower' case design. Also, CD-ROM drives installed on PCs in the network can usually be accessed by other PCs on the same network.**

HANDY TIP **Network users working from home can also access networked CDs by using programs like Microsoft's Dial-up Networking software supplied with Windows 95/ 98, providing the particular software licence permits this method of access.**

Achieving more with less using an Intranet

Intranets for example are one anticipated growth area. *A Web-based approach can provide one of the best ways in which to find and link related information.* An Intranet applies the same powerful navigation approach of the Internet to a private environment like a company Local Area Network (LAN). Users can then share and distribute information more easily making the job of communicating and working together more effective and more efficient.

Intranets are ideal for many users except for one aspect: to be effective and speed up decision making, it's important to keep the information available on an intranet up-to-date.

The 'traditional' network

A computer network can provide a range of facilities to the PCs in the network, such as printer and CD-ROM sharing, email and Internet access, group financial and marketing data, and group scheduling and diary services, to name but a few.

A collection of physically interconnected computers is known as a Local Area Network (LAN). Computers in different locations can be connected together to form a Wide Area Network (WAN).

In a LAN, usually, there is at least one powerful PC known as the server on which the central knowledge database is stored (ideally, have two servers running concurrently: one then 'mirrors' the other, so if one server goes down, the other takes over).

The file server

The file server is one of the central components of the network and runs the main network operating system, such as Microsoft Windows NT version 4.0 or the soon to be released and much hyped NT version 5.0.

The network operating system enables all the PCs and workstations to communicate with the server and each other, and controls the sharing of printers, modems, CD-ROM drives, and other peripheral devices.

REMEMBER

Network hubs don't usually contain any date-related components. But some of the more modern units may use dates. You need to establish whether these types of facility are crucial to your operations.

Clearly then, the file server is important. Here's a typical current specification for a file server: 300/333 MHz CPU, 256 Mb of Random Access Memory (RAM), an 8 Gbyte hard drive, a fast CD-ROM drive, a DAT high capacity backup tape drive (or an alternative disk-based backup system) and a fast Ethernet network card (10/100 Mbps speed). Finally, to reduce the possibility of virus infection, ideally install antivirus software on each server.

Network cabling and hubs

Near to each computer and peripheral device in the network is a wall point connection linking each device to the network cabling. Usually, the cabling is concealed within the building superstructure to preserve the office decor.

REMEMBER

Novell have released patches to ensure NetWare versions 3.12 and 4.10 are Year 2000 compliant. However, if you use NetWare, whatever version you use, check its Y2K status with your vendor: later updates may have been released.

Each device – eg, server, PC, workstation, printer, and such like – is able to communicate with the others on the network using network hubs. A hub allows a number of devices to be plugged into it, typically 8, 12 or 16. As the network expands, you can add more hubs as you need them to accommodate more devices.

Network cards

Most current generation network cards come in two speed flavours: 10 megabits per second (10BaseT) and 100 megabits per second (100BaseT). Ideally, choose network cards and hubs which transmit at 100 megabits per second to ensure data is moved around the network as fast as possible. Remember, 'mega' means 'million' and this speed equates to 100,000,000 bits each second: fast, whatever way you look at it!

Network PCs and workstations

A network PC can be a desktop or portable model and each has its own operation system, such as Windows 95/98 and

...cont'd

local hard drive. Any PC connected to a network can still use its own application software and directly connected printer, as well as using the resources on the network. A workstation uses the server operating system and does not usually contain hard disk storage.

An ideal network PC specification could include:

BEWARE

Local Area Networks (LANs) and Wide Area Networks (WANs) are even more vulnerable to the Year 2000 problem than single standalone PCs.

- 300 MHz Pentium CPU

- 64 Mbytes of RAM (at least)

- 3 Gbyte hard drive (at least)

- And a 10/100 Mbps Ethernet network card. A notebook PC requires a special type of network card connector called a PCMCIA or PC card

- Finally, to reduce the possibility of virus infection, ideally install antivirus software on each PC

HANDY TIP

Networking, although powerful, can be a complex business. To find out more, consider reading *Networking in easy steps*.

Backup security

By installing a mirrored server as described earlier, you can ensure you have the most cost effective access to your data at all times. Remember also, this way your data is stored in at least two separate locations (on each server). And as you backup your data at the end of each day, make sure you cycle different tapes, so that someone can keep at least one copy of the data off-site at all times. Then if the building housing your LAN burns down overnight, at least you'll still have your valuable and often irreplaceable data.

Protecting against power failure

It's not a bad idea to protect the server against power failures and power fluctuations. One of the best ways of doing this is to fit an Uninterruptible Power Supply (UPS) to each server. Then if the mains power supply to the network fails, a UPS can provide about 10–15 minutes of power to enable you to shut down normally without losing data.

If you perform a lot of printing you can also connect the printer to a UPS also.

Tapping the power of the Internet

To access the Internet and Web from any PC within an internal computer network, you can install Microsoft Proxy Server to provide shared Internet access. In this way, usage can limit access to only certain Web sites.

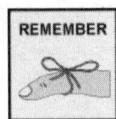

Consider using on-line banking facilities to reduce your costs. A recent Booz-Allen survey found that on average, the cost of a payment transaction was 10p for on-line banking, 36p when using the telephone, and 72p when using a high street branch.

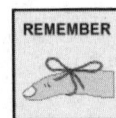

One estimate suggests sales from the Internet are set to reach £1.25 billion by 2000.

What is the Internet?

It's a vast network of interconnected computers spread across the globe, providing information, entertainment, business and research services, and much more. The Web is the most popular 'branch' of the Internet.

What's out there?

If you wanted, you could probably find information on almost every subject imaginable somewhere on the Internet. You can also send and receive emails and join in with others to discuss your favourite topics. But one of the most amazing realisations is that no one really owns the Internet.

Why is it so special?

Using the Internet, now ordinary men and women across the globe can present the same face as any trans-global corporation – and often succeed better.

The crystal ball: two-year sales projection

This is a time of enormous opportunity, in which anyone with a connection to the Internet has the potential to address millions. But don't wait too long. Currently, the Internet is not entirely a level playing field: it's biased towards those who are setting up their stall now or within the coming year.

The Internet is not a passing craze but a real business opportunity available to anyone. It has been hailed as the greatest leveller in history. Those who have found the gold are busy mining it. In a few years time, this king-sized window of opportunity will close and the advantages of being a forerunner will be lost. By that time, millions more will have realised the Internet's power and the amount of competition will have evened things out somewhat.

Get ready for the boom!

Let's look at one indicator: computers. With increased computer sales come all sorts of other sales, many not related in any way to computers. In 1996, £6,440,000,000 of computers and software was exported (Source: customs

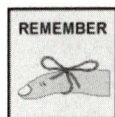

A Newsgroup is an Internet club in which people can take part in discussions, read articles, contribute, meet new friends, colleagues and business clients on-line. Tens of thousands of different newsgroups exist covering hundreds of special interest subjects.

To succeed on the Internet, it's important that your product or service has real, tangible 'must have' value.

The Internet offers an ideal way in which to monitor the activities of your competitors.

& Excise). In 1997, software and computing services rose by 19%, with over 9% average growth over the rest of the world. Arguably, these figures are just a hint of what is to come. Also remember, most new PCs now come with a modem and Internet access software as standard.

Many of these new buyers are going to go on-line for the first time simply to see what all the fuss is about. They'll have money to spend and once they become convinced it's safe to do so they'll often make savings by buying over the Internet instead of using traditional retail channels.

The UK picture

In Britain for example, there's much room for growth. Currently only 10.5% of UK homes has a computer. And now, PC prices are falling dramatically while PCs are easier to use than ever before. Increased computer sales also create other spin-offs, more software sales, accessories, even keyboard covers and wrist rests, to name but a few.

The secret's out

Lots of companies already exist on the Internet, selling a wide range of goods, yet they don't have offices, buildings, warehouses or inventory. They leave that to somebody else. And surprise surprise, of these 'virtual companies' many are rumoured to be making a great deal of money. Hardly surprising when the overheads are so low!

The point is, these amazing people have found new, better and more profitable ways in which to earn a living. Some Internet entrepreneurs are making enviable amounts of money through simply using email effectively. Many don't even need a Web site. Others use the Internet Newsgroups to make a valuable contribution and to gain new clients.

Most Web sites are not yet profitable. Some are beautifully designed with pages of attractive animated graphics but which simply don't make money. Key point: often the most successful Web sites adopt a plain, simple design that is focused on providing value to its customers, whether that be information, goods or services. An admirable approach!

Utilising the Web

HANDY TIP

Various promotions and incentives can be tested quickly and cost effectively on a Web site.

HANDY TIP

Some niche products often can't be sold cost effectively using 'traditional' approaches. However, these may be worth marketing on the Web (and Internet). The low setup and running costs of a Web site coupled with the powerful global reach can bring rich rewards.

HANDY TIP

For a Web page to succeed, ensure you create an effective, appropriate design. Consider the guidelines provided in *Web Page Design in easy steps*.

A Web page is like a kind of electronic magazine or brochure. The Web is now arguably the main branch of the Internet in which thousands of computers provide access to information and sell goods and services using Web pages. Here are some business-oriented benefits of establishing an effective Web presence:

- Exposure to millions worldwide. Provides a powerful global reach

- A Web page is a 'full attention' sales device. While someone is viewing your page, there's no competition

- Is a low cost, high visual impact advertising medium. You can use stunning full colour graphics, special effects like, flashing text, sound, voice and video files can be included if desired

- Web space is cheap and the overheads required to set up a Web site are low compared to more conventional business advertising-oriented practices

- Orders can be taken over the Internet using an email connection or directly through a secure Web page payment facility

- Your Web page works for you 24 hours a day, every day of the year

- Information can be easily changed and updated

- Set up an effective Web page and your status within the marketplace is immediately enhanced

- Your Web site 'address' can be included on all of your marketing materials, advertisements, stationery, etc.

- Provides another avenue for you to display your products or services

- For businesses and organisations, delivering a brochure on a Web site can save on conventional printing costs

Index

Y